WHERE
* WE *
# STAND

ALSO BY ROGER ROSENBLATT

Rules for Aging

Black Fiction

Children of War

Witness

Life Itself

Coming Apart

The Man in the Water

Consuming Desires

Roger Rosenblatt

WHERE

⋆ WE ⋆

STAND

30 Reasons for Loving Our Country

HARCOURT, INC.

New York   San Diego   London

www.HarcourtBooks.com

"Let Us Now Praise Famous Cities," "Everyone's a Liberal (Oh, Go Ahead, Read It Anyway)," and "I Guess We Let Anybody In" were originally published in different forms and under different titles in the *New York Times*.

"We Have a Very Well Written Constitution," "Our House Is a Very Very Very Fine House," "We Play Ball," "Annie Drops Her Gun (Smile When You Say That)," "But We're Extremely Disloyal," "We Are a Bunch of Losers, Ourselves," "We Shame Monsters," "We Dig That Hokey, Corny Presidential Talk," "Basically, We're Out of This World," "A River Runs Through Us," "Still Historical after All These Years," and "God Is Not on Our Side" were originally published in different forms and under different titles in *Time* magazine. © Time Inc. Used with permission.

Library of Congress Cataloging-in-Publication Data
Rosenblatt, Roger.
Where we stand: 30 reasons for loving our country/Roger Rosenblatt.—1st ed.
p.   cm.
ISBN 0-15-100722-5
1. National characteristics, American. 2. United States—Civilization.
3. United States—Civilization—Philosophy. 4. Social values—United States.
I. Title.
E169.1.R77556 2002
973—dc21   2002001753

Text set in Requiem
Designed by Cathy Riggs

Printed in the United States of America

First edition
A C E G I K J H F D B

For Jessica,
a brand new American

CONTENTS

* * *

WHERE
✴ WE ✴
STAND

PREFACE

✶ ✶ ✶

This book is about love of country—not unalloyed love, or unwary, unquestioning love, or infatuated, one-night, wink-in-the-bar love. But love, pure, steady, and complicated. I wrote it in a time when I found it useful to dredge up feelings about America that for a long time lay inside me. These feelings gave me comfort and resolve, and they are offered to you in hopes of the same. If you are put in the position of defending your way of life, as we have been, it may help to remember that we live in a pretty great country.

So, what follows is a collection of short essays, each on an aspect of American dreams and realities, that in aggregate attempt to make a case for preserving the core values of the country, along with all the oddities and nonsense that make us us. Some of the pieces are more confident than others. When I write about the brilliance of the Constitution, or the separation of church and state, I am a lot more certain that we have achieved what we sought to achieve than, say, when I write about poverty, race, or the treatment of children.

I don't spend a lot of words on the problematic issues, because they are well-known, and because I see them as unfinished business in a country that, sooner or later, has managed to deal with its unfinished business. These are the pillars of the Republic: to protect the weaker, to rescue the endangered, to dignify every individual, but, centrally, to continue the search for a more noble expression of existence. However we have blundered in the history of this search, it is where we stand.

Some of these essays discuss familiar rights and principles; some I've made up. There are pieces on why one is lucky (I should say blessed) to live in a place where no one version of God prevails. There are pieces about the beauty—and the lusty humor—of the old melting pot; about the absolute rights of those who are different from the majority; about the need to protect the freedom of authors and artists, especially the most offensive of these; and about the nuttiest excesses of freedom as well. Forgive me, but I also defend the existence of lawyers.

And there are some other values that occurred to me as I began to write: the "right" to lead a hard and complicated life; the "right" to mess up or improve our behavior; the "right" to be suspicious; the "right" to yearn, particularly for the unreachable; the "right" to be out of things, to laugh at our leaders, to lose, to dream, to drift.

Putting this book together taught me something. In the twenty-seven years or so that I have done this work, I have written essays about presidents, prisons, sports, the homeless, wars, books, movies, crooks, music, national foolishness, and other various subjects. I have drawn on many of these pieces here. But when I was writing them originally, I was wholly unaware that over the years another, larger, story in which they were all connected was writing itself in my mind. I had no idea how deep my admiration for my country went—no matter how often it was qualified. I had no idea that my affection was so strong. The process of writing was an extension of feelings stemming from September 11, when I teared up day after day. You too?

Anyway, the larger story is this book. The fact that it rose so rapidly and definitely in me suggests that a similar tale murmurs in you as well, in all of us who have shared the shaky joy of living in a very rare bird of a country. I am sure that the book contains some lulus of errors and porous arguments, and I know that it presents some fighting words. But it is the best I could do. The book was written because I felt like writing it, felt like saying anything I chose to say, and knew that I had the freedom to say it—if you get my drift.

ROGER ROSENBLATT

1

WE HAVE A VERY WELL WRITTEN CONSTITUTION

*In which the fellow who actually wrote the document
(no, it wasn't Jefferson or Madison) is finally given his due*

★ ★ ★

It helps to recognize that we were founded on a class document. When our Constitution was being made ready, the framers called upon a guy named Jacob Shallus to put it on paper—or parchment, actually. Shallus was an ordinary but skilled citizen, the son of a German immigrant, a soldier, a patriot, a father of eight, and, at the time of the Constitutional Convention, assistant clerk to the Pennsylvania General Assembly. The convention handed him the document for copying on September 15, 1787. The process was called "engrossing," which suggests a nice double meaning, and it meant copying the text out at an elegant angle in large, legible script.

Much of nature contributed to the enterprise. The four sheets of parchment were vellum, the skin of a lamb or calf, stretched, scraped, and dried. The ink was a blend of oak galls and dyes. The light by which he worked was probably an oil lamp. His instrument was a feather quill. Human nature was represented in the person of Shallus. He had forty hours to transfer 4,440 words to four sheets. For this assignment, the pay was thirty dollars, which wasn't bad money for moonlighting.

More than two centuries later, Shallus has become the answer to a trivia question, but the words he engrossed are given parades. What started out at one man's writing desk was eventually carried across the country from city to city as the nation's capital moved, was hidden during the War of 1812, was transferred from federal department to department until it wound up in the National Archives in Washington, sanctified in helium and watched over by an electronic camera conceived by NASA. The quill age became the space age, and at every stage, a nation full of grateful believers made a constant noisy fuss over a piece of writing barely the length of a short story with much theme, no plot, and characters implied.

Call the Constitution literature? Sarah Orne Jewett once wrote to Willa Cather, "The thing that teases the mind over and over for years, and at last gets itself put down rightly on paper . . . it belongs to literature." So the Constitution qualifies. Human minds were teased for centuries with the possibility of making a government that would allow that mind to realize itself. The document shows other literary attributes as well: a grounding in the ideas of its time, economy of language, orderliness, symmetrical design, a strong, arresting lead sentence. Then, there's all that shapely ambiguity. Even those who have never read the document are convinced that it foresaw all they endured—wars, debts, threats to health, privacy, and equality. A fantastic piece of work, it imagined a country full of people imagining themselves.

But I still love to picture Shallus, before any of these hopes were raised or satisfied, the four skins laid out before him, the ink, the quill, and the lamp. And the words, like mysterious ciphers, handed over to him by the best minds of the age, who had just sweated out a Philadelphia summer to claim the intellectual territory that was to translate to a civilization. Did Shallus read what he had copied when he finished? Would he have understood it if he had? How could he have dreamt that all those words, thought through so meticulously, were conceived only for him?

2

WE ARE FREE TO BE YOU, ME,
STUPID, AND DEAD

In which the author defends your right to say anything,
no matter how awful, as long as it is not about him

✳ ✳ ✳

Everyone loves free expression as long as it isn't exercised. Several years ago, Mahmoud Abdul-Rauf, a basketball player for the Denver Nuggets, refused to stand up for the playing of the national anthem because of personal religious convictions. The National Basketball Association greeted his decision by suspending him from the league until someone suggested that the Founding Fathers had actually meant it when they allowed someone to do something that would outrage the rest of us.

Similarly, major league baseball suspended John Rocker, the famous nutcase relief pitcher for the Atlanta

Braves, when Rocker said that he did not want to ride New York City's Number 7 subway with all those single moms, queers, and illegal aliens. The court did not interfere, perhaps because the Constitution only states that government has no right to prevent free expression; it grants no affirmative licenses. I don't really get the difference between the two cases, but I know that Rocker had a perfect, or rather imperfect, right to sound like a jackass.

The rights of jackasses are more than a national staple. The strange beauty of American freedom is that it is ungovernable, that it always runs slightly ahead of human temperament. You think you know what you will tolerate. A man on a soapbox speaks out for China. Fine. An editorial calls for sympathy with the Taliban. (Gulp) okay. But then a bunch of Nazis want to march around Skokie, Illinois, or Harlem, and, hold on a minute! And what the hell is this? An art exhibit called "African-American Flag" in New Jersey. Or this? An exhibit in the Phoenix Art Museum called "What Is the Proper Way to Display the U.S. Flag?"

Now that one was a doozie. The exhibit required observers to walk across an American flag on the floor to get to what was displayed on a wall. "That's my flag, and I'm going to defend it," said a visitor to the museum as he tried to take the flag from the floor. "No son of a bitch is going to do that."

The thing that I like best about sons of bitches doing that and worse, as long as they do not cry "fire" in a crowded flag, is: (a) it enhances my appreciation of the wild courage of the Founders, and (b) it expands my mind, which could use some expanding. Freedom is like a legal drug. *How far will we go?* is not a rhetorical question here. Another exhibit in Chicago showed a flag with the word "think" where the stars should have been. Think. I hate it when that happens.

You think you know how far freedom will go in America, and then you meet another jackass. In the 1990s, I wrote a story for the *New York Times Magazine* about the Philip Morris company called "How Do They Live with Themselves?" The answer to that question, which came from the company executives I interviewed, turned out to be "Quite comfortably, thanks." The reason that their consciences did not seem to bother them about manufacturing an addictive lethal product was that their customers were engaging in the blessed American activity of freedom of choice. They were right—at least until new laws or lawsuits would prove them wrong. People technically had the choice of becoming addicted to cigarettes or not. I doubt that any of the Philip Morris people would ever step on the flag.

Since free is the way people's minds were made to be, it has been instructive for me to spend time in places where freedom was limited. In the Soviet Union, it was fascinating to see how many ways the workers of the world managed to squeeze free thought through the cracks of their utopian cells: The secret publication of books, the pirated music, the tricky subversive lines of poetry read at vast gatherings of tens of thousands. And the below-the-surface comedy. I was checking out of a hotel in Tbilisi. Checking out of Russian hotels was always a feat—they didn't have dollars, they didn't have rubles, no one had ever checked out before. The clerk at the desk spoke little English, and she wanted to tell me that another, more fluent, clerk would be along shortly. "Mr. Rosenblatt," she said. "Would you mind coming back in fifteen years?" We both exploded in laughter because we knew it was remotely possible.

The mind expands, the mind settles, then is shaken

up, resists, and expands again. One of the great ongoing stupidities of the country are school boards and library committees that ban certain books they deem dangerous. On the positive side, though, the folks who do the banning offer some delightful defenses for their decisions. The three literary works most frequently banned in our country are *Macbeth, King Lear,* and *The Great Gatsby.* The reason school boards offer for banning *Macbeth* is that the play promotes witchcraft. Perhaps it does. One doesn't think of *Macbeth* as promoting things, but if it did, witchcraft would be it. They don't say why they want to ban *King Lear.* Promotes ingratitude, I suppose. I assume that *The Great Gatsby* promotes Long Island.

Sometimes the reasons offered for censoring certain works are obscure, thus intriguing. In Georgia, the Harry Potter books were recently burned because they were said to encourage kids to want to be sorcerers. In Spokane, Washington, they wanted to remove the children's picture book *Where's Waldo?* from the elementary school library. People objected to *Where's Waldo?,* they said, because it contains "explicit subject matter." A plea for surrealism, I imagine. In Springfield, Virginia, they banned a book called *Hitler's Hang-Ups* because it offered "explicit sexual details about Hitler's life." Given the *other* tendencies of Hitler's life, I should think the sexual details would be relatively acceptable. And, in the town of Astoria, Oregon, a book called *Wait Till Helen Comes* was challenged in an elementary school for giving "a morbid portrayal of death." Now they've gone too far.

3

WE'RE DIGNIFIED. THAT'S WHAT
I SAID—DIGNIFIED

*In which the preposterous idea is put forward that
we are not as vulgar as we think we are*

* * *

Dignity can be a nasty little word, especially when it is used to imply that someone who shows it is better than the people he's generally associated with. A compliment to an individual can wind up reinforcing an insult to a group. When a member of a minority is called dignified, watch out. It can sound very much like the word "articulate," so I try to avoid it.

No longer. The fact is that most Americans—contrary to reputation—conduct themselves with a considerable amount of dignity most of the time. Dignity arises in a country where work is centrally important and is therefore shown by people simply going about their jobs.

One of the painful beauties that emerged from September 11 was the dignity shown by firefighters, policemen, nurses, rescue workers, volunteers, and many others. I should say reemerged, since these folks were doing work that always had dignity, and heroism, built into it. Dignity showed in their attitude toward their tasks, in the sympathy they extended to one another, in their solemn respect for the dead. No one who watched the workers remove their hardhats and open a column of space for the flag-covered bodies will ever forget it.

There was the dignity shown by Mayor Rudy Giuliani as well, who seemed wholly in control of the deepest feelings of the moment. If anyone ever doubted that a public servant's private life need have no bearing on his civic performance, Giuliani proved it. He handled himself coolly, but his best characteristic was that he understood that dignity also means sympathy for others. When reporters questioned him about how many people were killed, he answered, "We don't know the numbers, but we know it will be unbearable."

There was also the dignity of the mourners—those whose lives were rent by the attacks. They spoke not of anger or revenge, but of the virtues of the people they would miss in the ever-lengthening absence that death creates. That dignity continued to be displayed when some of the women who were widowed testified before Congress about not having received enough money to live on. Here was good old American protest by ordinary citizens, not by big shots, quietly but definitely speaking up for their rights.

We have been so stupefied in recent years with our celebrity-crazy value system that we have forgotten the significance of the ordinary citizen, the person who was once known honorably as "the common man." In the eighteenth century, he was the subject of Gray's "Elegy Written in a Country Churchyard." In the nineteenth century, he was a farmer, the man with the hoe. In the twentieth, he was the ordinary Joe, sometimes the G.I. Joe, Bill Mauldin's pair of cartoon soldiers. The common man, though hardly perfect, was the essential American. He could be beaten down, and he could do the beating. The hardhats of the 1960s—with whom the student anti-war movement tried pathetically (and often comically) to ally itself—often acted against minorities and women.

Nonetheless, the common man and woman remain the American ideal, even when we forget to mention them, as we have until recently. In our touching hypocrisy, all of us want to be rich, powerful, and ordinary at the same time. The regular guy is exalted because, flaws aside, he is assumed to have a code of honor as well as a work ethic. It is he who stabilizes society, yet who also changes it for the better. All revolutions start from the bottom up.

In his essay, "What I Believe," E. M. Forster wrote:

> I believe in aristocracy. Not an aristocracy of power, based upon rank and influence, but an aristocracy of the sensitive, the considerate and the plucky. Its members represent the true human tradition, the one permanent victory of our queer race over cruelty and chaos. They are sensitive for others as well as for themselves, they are considerate without being fussy, their pluck is not swankiness but the power to endure, and they can take a joke.

Forster's definition is nicely democratic, but its special accuracy lies in its three components of praiseworthy conduct. By "pluck" he means endurance of the sort that neither swaggers nor dresses itself in Hamlet's black. By "considerate" he means the exercise of just enough attention to others to display genuine feeling, but not so much as to be cloying. It is significant that he names sensitivity first. To be sensitive within oneself and for the benefit of others—that is an aristocrat. Implied, too, in Forster's way of thinking is what the aristocrats of the spirit are not—cheap, whiny, petty. They are without showiness, without envy, without narrowness of any kind. They do have certain snobberies. They look down on bullies, bigots, and cheats. Their idea of lowlife is a gossip, and the commoners they snub are the cruel, the ungenerous, and the unkind.

All these qualities have been in evidence on so many levels since September 11. And they have not been confined to the obscure, either. The Yankees' Derek Jeter was one of hundreds of well-known people who visited Ground Zero, raised money for the victims, or otherwise showed what the country is made of. Baseball hero Jeter called the workers "the real heroes." Celebrities may be dazzling as celebrities, but they only make their way into our hearts when they show themselves to be regular folks.

Perhaps the most heartrending display of dignity came from families of those lost in the war so far. I am always amazed at the ease with which everybody appears on television these days. I think that it is due to camcorders; anyone can do it. But not everyone can do it right. The aristocracy of spirit shown by the parents of

Nathan Ross Chapman, the first American soldier killed by enemy fire in early January, was completely human. Chapman's father talked of their son's sense of duty, and his mother faltered a little when she considered whether the cause was worth the death of her boy. They said a few soft words, and that was that.

4

BUT WE'RE EXTREMELY DISLOYAL

*In which the loyalty of such Americans as Ronald Reagan,
John Dean, George McGovern, Rose Mary Woods,
and Benedict Arnold is called into question*

✶ ✶ ✶

Generally, Americans know when to be loyal to their leaders—and when not to be. After September 11, only someone looking to be intellectually cute or perverse would have turned his or her back on the nation under attack. But not long after September 11, when Attorney General John Ashcroft and others began to speak of military tribunals, interferences with normal civil liberties such as lawyer-client confidences, and the detaining of suspects without evidence, no one thought it disloyal for the nation to keep an eye on our own principles.

One of the delights of this country is that it has disloyalty built into its system. This is because the intelligently disloyal subject knows when to go against the grain and when to harvest it. But it is also because Americans have a sophisticated understanding about loyalty—that it is impossible to achieve consistently. In some ways, disloyalty is an acknowledgment of reality. Auden had it right in the poem "Lullaby": "Lay your sleeping head, my love / Human on my faithless arm." Ah, humans.

Sooner or later, in big things or small, everybody lets everybody down—not necessarily out of malice, but because loyalty runs counter to what one laughingly calls normal human behavior. "Into what danger would you lead me, Cassius?" asks Brutus, who is, in fact, an honorable man yet is easily seduced to treason by an envious one. I can still hear George McGovern's avowal of fealty to his running mate, Thomas Eagleton, in the 1972 presidential campaign after it was revealed that Eagleton had undergone electric-shock therapy. "I'm behind him, one thousand percent," said McGovern, a few days before dumping him.

I have always suspected that a bank with "Fidelity" in its title was going to lose my money. The mere assertion of loyalty is often enough to signal betrayal. One of the weaknesses of loyalty is that, unlike friendship, it requires some outward demonstration or declaration and so invites insincerity. It is also, by implication, unconditional and suggests that though you do not agree with the person or institution to which you are expected to stick, you will do so anyway. All this practically guarantees treason.

This is not to suggest that one ought to be disloyal promiscuously or without making an effort toward steadfastness. Yet as noble a standard as loyalty sets, there is simply too much fear, self-doubt, opportunism, ambition, or plain old critical disapproval in our makeup to expect anyone to adhere to it. How many loyal free-agent ballplayers can one name, or publishing executives, or authors? How many loyal corporations these days? How's Enron doing? When it comes to matrimonial vows, "I do" is a promise that sometimes lasts until the first Finnair hostess swings down the aisle.

In his book defending the Clinton years, *Stickin': The Case for Loyalty,* James Carville notes that more people turn on presidents than stick with them—though there are ways of doing both, as Peter Edelman of the Department of Health and Human Services proved when he waited for the passage of Clinton's welfare bill before resigning because he could not stomach it. He was acting out of principled thinking, which is what most of us try to do when deciding to support or protest our government. But whatever one's reasons, total constancy to the ideal is not useful. *A Few Good Men* was about the potential inhumanity of too much Semper Fi. Even dogs, to whom we assign unswerving devotion, will, because they are dogs, bite the hands that feed them.

So unachievable is the goal of absolute loyalty that it is usually the betrayals that make life in America and elsewhere interesting. (See John Dean and Nixon; David Stockman and Reagan; Judas and Jesus.) If Archibald Cox had stuck by Nixon, we would have been stuck with him. To be sure, there are people famous for loyalty, but they are often loyal to a fault, and a supposed virtue becomes pathetic, stupid, sometimes criminal. Rose Mary Woods entered history when she stood by her man's tape recorder. Hubert Humphrey probably lost the presidency when he stuck by Lyndon Johnson and his Vietnam policies. Then there was Mrs. Odysseus.

To appreciate how crazy loyalty can get, recall Shoichi Yokoi, the World War II Japanese soldier who hid in the jungles of Guam for twenty-seven years rather than surrender to U.S. forces. He had declared fidelity to Emperor Hirohito and had evidently meant it.

The best manifestations of loyalty occur in situations such as ours right now. We saw it in the camaraderie of the people in the military. We see it in the rescue workers at Ground Zero. So passionate were the feelings of the firefighters toward their slain brothers that for a bitter public moment they openly fought with their fellow-rescuers over the ceasing of recovery efforts. We see it in ourselves—in reflexes rising out of pride in what the country has achieved, what it represents, the general great good sense of its people. And we also see it in our decision not to be excessive about it, so that we are not automatically loyal to our leaders, since that would constitute a betrayal of the country.

The worst manifestations of loyalty occur when the government attempts to mandate actions by using phrases such as "the national interest" without explanation (J.F.K. kept journalists silent with that trick) or with loyalty oaths. During the McCarthy shame, graduate students were required to sign loyalty oaths when they applied for government grants. A dean at Harvard defended this practice as being merely pro forma—of no greater significance, he said, than licking the stamps on the application envelopes. At a faculty meeting, the great Italian scholar Renato Poggioli stood up and commented, "Mr. Dean, I am from Fascist Italy, and I will tell you something. First you licka the stamps, then you licka something else."

5

Everyone's a Liberal (Oh, Go Ahead and Read It Anyway)

In which the author picks a fight with conservatives, including his old man

✷ ✷ ✷

My father was a wonderful man but he was very conservative, and when I was young, much of our time together was spent in political warfare. I, the conventional liberal, was always in the right in these battles, but my father won every argument, partly because he was smarter than I and partly because you don't have to scratch a conservative too hard in America to disclose a disappointed liberal, hopeful as ever, muttering beneath the surface. So my father could have our fights both ways. Example:

He and I were watching the evening news one night when George Wallace came on. This was in the mid-1960s, when the former governor of Alabama was in his heyday of race-baiting—before he got shot and became a national treasure. That night he was flinging his customary rant about how the "nigras" ought to be kept separate from whites and how separate meant equal— the usual horseshit—as my father and I watched in our customary stony silence. Wallace went on for four or five minutes. It seemed interminable. Finally, he stopped. My father waited just the right beat. "You know," he said at last, "in a decent world, a jackass like that wouldn't be given ten seconds on television. But thanks to you liberals, he can talk his brains out."

Apart from illustrating my typical defeat, the story suggests a proposition that I realize will be offensive to conservatives, but is, I believe, nonetheless generally true about American political opinion: We are basically a nation of liberals. Like my dad, most conservatives are far more liberal than they make out and only get gruff about liberal excesses after they have been—in former-liberal Irving Kristol's famous phrase—"mugged by reality." But that mugging, which resulted in the creation of most neo-conservatives in the 1960s, also served to alert us liberals to our own foolishness. Thanks to us liberals—as

Irving Kristol and my father knew perfectly well—this country is a continually, if reluctantly, improving entity.

The America I heard singing when I was a teenager in the late 1950s forced homosexuals into hiding, ignored or derided the disabled, withheld rights from suspects of crimes, and kept women in their place, which was usually the kitchen and sometimes an abortionist's back room. It foisted prayers on schoolchildren, paid no attention to the health needs of the impoverished or the elderly, endangered endangered species, and threw people out of work because they held what was considered to be an un-American ideology. In certain states, it denied black Americans the right to sit where they wished to on a public bus, to drink from a public water fountain, to eat in restaurants, stay in hotels, go to public schools with whites, or vote. Tell kids all this today, and they think I'm talking about another country. I am.

Every one of these conditions has been corrected or improved by laws and attitudes derived from a philosophy that is held in such low esteem these days that the worst insult one political candidate can fling at another is to call him or her a liberal. What is interesting about these kinds of attacks is that underneath it all, they take their energy from the presumption that liberalism is robust and established. They are right. Americans have never hated big government as much as we have loved its services. But our feelings go beyond self-interest. We have accepted, indeed embraced, the national obligation to help the young, the elderly, the ill, the poor, and the generally disadvantaged. This is sometimes difficult to prove, but as was said in the O. J. Simpson trial, the absence of evidence is not evidence of absence. If recent Democratic platforms look Republican, it is not because the Democrats have abandoned the liberal agenda but because the Republicans have absorbed it.

The liberalism I am thinking of is a kind of general cultural-political liberalism, a mixture of the New Deal programs of the 1930s and the individual-rights movements of the 1960s, which knocked the wind out of the callous, restrictive, and narrow-minded conditions I grew up with a few decades ago. It is a malleable philosophy, generous and socially responsible, that governs how people ought to live with one another in a healthy democracy. It is not the specific liberalism of the Franklin Roosevelt era, or the Lyndon Johnson era, or explicitly that of voting-rights laws or expanded civil liberties, though it creates and encourages such developments. Rather, it is the sentiment that may be traced back to our first principles, that people are inherently equal, that they have a right to pursue their individuality in an open society, and that the state must use its power and authority to secure their rights and to help the needier among them.

In its competition with ultraconservative thinking for the soul of America, this liberalism has won hands down. So why does it seem defeated? Because the ruckus that has been raised against it in recent years has been countered by little or no persuasive defense. (Heywood Broun had it right too often: "A liberal is a man who leaves the room when the fight begins.") Because there have been a number of substantial right-wing victories or near-victories involving such issues as homosexual rights, book and press censorship, and flag-burning. Because public figures like Pat Robertson, Ralph Reed, Pat Buchanan, and Newt Gingrich and right-wing talk-show hosts like G. Gordon Liddy and Rush Limbaugh who oppose one or another element of liberal thought are more colorful and draw more attention than do their opponents. Because liberalism has no true leader. And because it has shot itself in the foot. Through careless statements and errors of omission it has misrepresented both its intelligence and its sense of civic responsibility.

Given liberalism's success, it is remarkable how lily-livered we liberals have appeared when attacked. In the interests of fostering open-mindedness, we've allowed the misimpression to be shouted abroad that we have no standards of taste, morality, educational values, spiritual and community life, or common sense. Political correctness, often properly called a fundamentalism of the left, is a bitter joke to all but those who practice it. In a cultural atmosphere in which liberals are assumed to support the purveyors of sacrilege and dirty talk, the purveyors of simple-minded virtue, like William Bennett, come off as moral leaders, and the public has a choice between the tasteless and the boring.

In fact, most liberals who favor the protections of an open society are appalled by its excesses, but we have not made that clear. To my way of thinking, the only thing an art exhibit of a urine-soaked Jesus has going for it is the right to be shown. Liberals have appeared to be crazy about every subculture except that of married, hardworking, homebuying, churchgoing Americans. We have dwelt on small-potato infringements like the raising of crèches and menorahs in public squares. A main-stay of liberalism, the separation of church and state, has taken the odd form of a disregard of, and disrespect for, religion. The notion that liberals are anti-religion has emboldened the crackpot intolerance of the religious right.

Yet the fact remains that for all of liberalism's mis-steps and inadequacies, America has signed on for it. There are major areas of activity, like rights for women, the handicapped, minorities, and the environment, that could not have changed the American landscape without great numbers of people agreeing that they wanted gov-ernment in their lives. Ask anyone who goes to an air-port these days if he wants government out of the security business. Ask anyone if he wants to abandon FDR's four freedoms, especially freedom from fear. Ask anyone what was really attacked on September 11. Our free, sauntering, fair-minded, kindhearted, adventurous, creative, unbridled, unorthodox, unimaginable liberal life—that's what.

By now, I suppose that you conservatives reading this have steam shooting out of your ears. Sorry. But we're in the same bouncing boat. The truth of liberalism is that it is both optimistic and pragmatic. It believes in improvement but not in perfectibility. It is often embarrassed by the freedoms it supports and encourages and by the occasionally unwieldy government it promotes. But it believes in the dream of human nobility, which historically has proved equally fanciful and reasonable. This is the conservative dream as well. I miss my dad.

6

GOD IS NOT ON OUR SIDE

In which one is invited to consider whether He is or is not,
or She is or is not, or whether one can know or not know,
or should know or should not—or not

✴ ✴ ✴

One of the more lethal and dangerous beliefs a people can hold is that God is on their side, which is why Americans are blessed, because God isn't. Or if He is (I'll stay with He), one has no way of knowing that He is—unless, of course, one is like Mohamed Atta, one of the terrorists in the attacking airplanes, who had a pathological view of faith, or Jerry Falwell, whose mind is Taliban minus the bloodlust. The Taliban leader, Mohammed Omar, may be wondering how tight he was with God after all. On September 11 he was certain that God rooted for our extinction. When Kandahar surrendered, the mullah may have gone shopping around for a more competent deity.

"A fanatic," said Finley Peter Dunne's Mr. Dooley, "is a man that does what he thinks th' Lord wud do if He knew th' facts in th' case." On the other hand, there are folks like me who are fanatically *uncertain* about what God is thinking. I believe in Him, all right. But I have no way of knowing that He is on our, or any, side in wars or that He oversouls his way through the trees or that He presides over my bowling game. The whole original reason for our separation of church and state was not simply to prevent a state religion but also to make a preemptive strike at the consequences of having a state religion—the deadliest of which being the assumption that God is on our side.

The essential act of faith, it seems to me, is wonder—a sort of involuntary fascination in awe. The Founding Fathers would approve of this sort of belief, I think. They respected various religions, but they also knew that religions are by nature limiting. William F. Buckley Jr. once quipped that Catholicism was his favorite religion. Mine is Judaism. What would one expect? Religions are concerned with ideology, uniformity, loyalty, and favoritism. Anyone can say that he respects someone else's religion, but it is like saying he thinks someone else's children are wonderful.

Similarly, if one prays for gifts and protections, one must naturally assume that God micromanages the universe for the advantage of particular believers. If, however, one sees prayer as what theologian Paul Tillich called "the great deep sigh," prayer becomes an act of unconscious adoration. Religion becomes more generous and modest. Even the Gospels were written "according to," which was a way of saying "as I see it." America is the most religious country in the industrialized world, and the reason for that may be because we see religion essentially as private property.

One would like to believe that God is on our side against the terrorists, because the terrorists are wrong and we are in the right, and any deity worth his salt would be able to discern that objective truth. I, too, want to believe that God is on our side or, as someone once hoped, that we are on His. But how can I know this? The claim is simply good-hearted optimism cloaked in morality—the same kind of thinking that makes people decide that God created humans in His own image. (See the old *New Yorker* cartoon that shows a giraffe in a field, thinking "And God made giraffe in his own image.") The

God worth worshiping is the one who pays us the compliment of self-regulation, much like the federal government does most of the time, and we might return the compliment by minding our own business.

In practical terms, it might be quite upsetting to learn God's opinion on such issues as human cloning, abortion, school prayer, capital punishment, conservation, nuclear weapons, starvation, disease, and an excessive number of Krispy Kremes. Where has God been since 1973 regarding the New York Knicks? I'd like to know. If one wants proof that God does not side with someone who merely invokes his name frequently, take point guard Charlie Ward—please.

This whole business of knowing God's devices is particularly nettling to us modern scientific Americans who have assured ourselves that we are capable of knowing everything. But it is always interesting to see how knowledge, no matter how fundamental or revolutionary, discloses as many mysteries as it unravels. One reason that religion thrives in America may be that we see the whole country as a religion—a construct of faith that encourages belief and wonder simultaneously.

Theologian Dietrich Bonhoeffer made his way to America from Nazi Germany at the outbreak of World

War II but then decided to return to his country to join the Resistance. He participated in a failed attempt to assassinate Hitler and was caught, jailed, and hanged. Bonhoeffer addressed this question of knowing with the example of a rose. He said that science allows us to grasp nearly everything about the composition of a rose because we have learned so much about pollination, photosynthesis, and so forth. And yet, once we have done all that analysis, we still ask, What is a rose?

Hitler had a different question. "Who says," he asked, "that I am not under the special protection of God?"

7

A RIVER RUNS THROUGH US

*In which we're exhilarated and scared to
death as we round the bend*

★ ★ ★

Mark Twain placed Huck and Jim on the river because the river was time, motion, beauty, baptism, and
violence, but mainly because they could not see around
the bend and still had the courage to keep going. Civi-
lizations are formed by bends in the river—the Nile, the
Congo, the Thames, the Yangtze—twists of land, water,
and fate that, by making it impossible to see what comes
next, raise hopes of the possibility of everything. We are
at a bend in the river right now; in our campaign against
terrorism we have entered into a conflict that will indicate where we want to go in terms of foreign policy, rules
of engagement, international law and alliances, along with
a ton of domestic decisions. Every time we are put in the

position of daring something and of learning something, we're at a bend in the river, which offers hope and fear in the same waters.

The Mississippi did that from the start. In the spring and summer of 1768, Montfort Browne, governor of British West Florida, made his way along the lower Mississippi to the area of "the Natches," where he found "the most charming prospects in the world." By the mid-1770s, colonial explorers were following rivers everywhere into the country—rivers with Indian names, which allowed progress and also enabled the latest Americans to kill off the first ones. They came from central and western New York by way of the Ohio; from Maryland and Virginia by way of the Tennessee; from western North Carolina through the Appalachian Mountains to the Tennessee and Mississippi valleys, following the rivers for hundreds of miles, which allowed the old world to flow into the new.

A river runs through us. The bend in the river is a story about to be disclosed; it offers the future and tests the will to enter that future, which is also a test of whom we wish to be—a test that we usually, eventually, pass, and that, in any event, we always have the nerve to take.

American artists have written, sung, painted, and even gone round the bend, gone mad, in the name of rivers. In his overboard essay on Huck and Jim, Leslie Fiedler wrote that the river supports "the American dream of isolation afloat." Out of that isolation in motion comes every inspiration, from contemplation (Langston Hughes's "The Negro Speaks of Rivers") to adventure (Hemingway's stories) to despair. The poet John Berryman looked down into the Mississippi and jumped to his death. The river is expanse, but it is also loneliness; Huck finds a loving relationship with Jim, but he is alone in his moral predicament. The American rivers show us a country equally capable of generosity and advancement, of glorying in and drowning in freedom, and of immense courage in the name of right.

Ever since the Jordan, people have used rivers to find something. But in America rivers have meant more than quests and more than entrances or borders. They have been tests of what the country wanted of its wilderness and of itself—reminders of the beckoning wilderness of the American mind. Water seems always to be where the great national story unfolds—Melville's ocean, Dreiser's lake, Fitzgerald's bay. But as Twain suggested, nothing was ever as deep as the river. The Atlantic becomes transformed into endless boulevards that run back and forth, offering both the allure and the illusion of eternity.

They have served as the passageways to killing grounds and tyrannies, where the "dark" people have been slaughtered or subdued by the children of "the light." As agents of social mobility they have allowed robust expansions, both vertical and horizontal. They have opened America to its imagination. They have invited exploitation of the natural conditions around them and of themselves—dammed up, dried up. They have allowed for collective and individual moral choice: kill or don't kill. Enslave or set everyone free.

Everything the river offers turns on the idea of America as Eden—an idea that we don't take as seriously as we pretend to, and yet it is no less enchanting to us than it was to the colonists. The country finds Eden; the country loses Eden; the country yearns for Eden. This is what happened before, during, and after September 11, and it is what always happens here. In *Life on the Mississippi,* Twain described his early infatuation with the river's beauty at sunset: "A broad expanse of the river was turned to blood; in the middle distance the red hue brightened into gold through which a solitary log came floating, black and conspicuous; in one place a long, slanting mark lay sparkling upon the water; in another the surface was broken by boiling, tumbling rings, that were as many-tinted as an opal."

Like Adam, he exulted, "the world was new to me." And then he lamented that "a day came when I began to cease noting the glories and the charms which the moon and the sun and the twilight wrought upon the river's face." Yet when he came to write his novel, all the original wonder returned to him: "Once or twice at night we would see a steamboat slipping along in the dark, and now and then she would belch a whole world of sparks up out of her chimbleys, and they would rain down in the river and look awful pretty; then she would turn a corner and her lights would wink out and the powwow shut off and leave the river still again."

America lies around the bend in the river, but it is the bend itself that determines the country's worth. Somewhere in that curve is the capacity to long for the best, to screw things up royally, and then to start over and do it right. Somewhere, too, is Lethe, the river of forgetfulness in which no lesson takes hold. The river carries the country into its sin and grandeur and magnificent contradictions. Now it carries us into a war with the terrible consequences of all wars, but a necessary nightmare if we are to preserve the freedoms we believe in. Deciding to liberate Jim and himself, Huck says, "All right, then, I'll go to hell"—referring to salvation.

8

I Guess We Let Anybody In

*In which we do, and enjoy highlights and a makeover
at the Hello Gorgeous Beauty Salon*

✴ ✴ ✴

Felix Iosifovich Andreev is having a rough day. Because he is executive director of the Brighton Beach District Management Association, because he calls himself the unofficial "mayir" of the neighborhood, because he is a natural-born promoter and something of an apparatchik, and because he grew up in Moscow, his head teeming with "wild dreams" of America as the land of "liberty and generous people," he wants nothing more than to show off Brighton Beach as a model of American immigrant life. He is dismayed when it turns out to be just that.

He is still too green a citizen to know that American immigrant life, especially in New York where it is most lavishly displayed, asserts its character by letting people down as soon as it bucks them up and that this jostling continues until they awaken one morning to discover that they have turned up in the country of their dreams. This has been particularly true in Brooklyn, which since the 1850s has cooked and stirred a psychedelic soup of Irish, Germans, Italians, Poles, African-Americans, Scandinavians, Puerto Ricans, and, more recently, Dominicans, Mexicans, Central Americans, Middle Easterners, Asians, and now the people of Felix Andreev. The earlier arrivals crowded onto Ellis Island; the latest ones swoop into Kennedy Airport, their dreams submerged by weariness, bewilderment, and open-faced excitement. Andreev's dreams rise from deep in his own quite unenigmatic Russian soul. He is the American immigrant Everyman, rolled into one hard-bellied, bald, bearded, fifty-five-year-old, former boxer's body. And he is all expectation.

But today, when he desperately wants to present his Brighton Beach paradise to me in the rosiest light and some of his fellow residents are behaving like a lower order of angels, the round, expectant, happy face of Felix Andreev droops. The owner of Empire Optical on Brighton Beach Avenue is a surly twenty-six-year-old who arrived at sixteen and answers all questions with a disgusted shrug, as if any subject other than the selling of eyeglasses is a waste of time.

"What surprises you most about this country?" I ask him.

"Nothing."

"What do you like best or least about it?"

"I work. That's it."

"You don't like it here?"

"It's all right." He turns away toward a customer.

Outside, Andreev shouts to make himself heard over the clacking of the El, which is the continuous background noise of the neighborhood. He is mortified. "I don't understand his attitude," he says, glancing back at the shop window with the frown of an injured parent. "What's he have to be sour about?" He walks a few steps between Fifth and Sixth Streets. "Ah, here." He points out a store that sells hardware, glassware, and fancy dishes. "Gennadi will be a different story," which he is and is not. Gennadi is thirty-nine. He came from Odessa (as did almost half of the 50,000 Brighton Beach–area residents) in 1975. Unlike the optician, he is gracious and shyly friendly and "feels more American than Russian, because here you get what you want to get, learn what you wish to learn." At the same time, he is appalled by the level of crime. His store has been robbed twice. "I am afraid for my kids."

Andreev gives me a driving tour of the area, which is not large; the beach extends about a mile and a half, with fifteen tributary streets leading down to it. Puffing up again, he points out the mixture of other ethnic groups—Koreans, Turks, Arabs. A man from Tashkent sits enthroned in his fabric and yarn store, serene as an oracle in his white beard and black *tubeteíka,* an Oriental skullcap. Next to shops that advertise themselves in Cyrillic are Chinese takeouts, pizzerias, and, perhaps the best-named establishment on earth, the Hello Gorgeous Beauty Salon.

It is an entire old world, or two old worlds in one. Except for the beach—the extraordinary boulevards of boardwalk and sand that attracted millions of vacationing families as recently as fifty years ago—the neighborhood is an odd mixture of Art Deco apartment houses with summer names like Mira-Mar, and drab, gray-white apartment houses like those on the outskirts of St. Petersburg. Here sunbathers lounged in Adirondack chairs, the world's best one-wall handball was played, Milton Berle and Lionel Hampton entertained, and Neil Sedaka, a native, was inspired to write the music to "Love Will Keep Us Together." Now, strangely, all this looks like

Russia: the chatter, the gossip, the lines at the markets, the awkward hipness of the teenagers, the generally drab dress of the elders. The beach itself resembles the wide beach at Riga in Latvia, though the sand is not so hard and dark. Old women in babushkas, muttering men, and a snuggling couple or two hunker down on the benches that face the sea.

The other old world in Brighton Beach is turn-of-the-century European immigrant America, where people were as energetic and optimistic as Andreev wishes them to be and as curt as the young optician. The differences between Brighton Beach and that former world are that the Brighton Beach of today is middle class, not poor; that the people who came here in the late 1980s, unlike their Ellis Island counterparts, entered a welfare state; that they can (and sometimes do) fly back to visit the real old country in a few hours.

"The blessing of America," Andreev exults, "is that you work for what you get, and what you get, you keep."

But reality slaps him down again as we approach the Babi Yar memorial, a small, not-quite-triangular park normally for kids but filled at midday with grumpy, furtive, down-and-out domino players. Andreev strides toward them, scooping up the air with his arms to encourage them to be open and friendly. They spit on the ground and respond with expletives, then turn their backs to him and go on with their game. He implores them; they show him only scorn. "They are ashamed," he explains, as if we are witnessing an anthropological phenomenon. "They do not want to be caught playing dominoes when they should be out looking for work."

Public relations begin to look up for Andreev when we go to lunch at a Georgian restaurant, and a young waiter tells me, "When I'm not working in the restaurant, I'm taking classes in English. And there is a—what—spiritual satisfaction? At the end of the day I know that I have earned something. And if I earn enough, I won't have to be a waiter forever. I'll open my own bar and restaurant. Yes." He nods for emphasis. "I would like to do that."

Andreev is beaming at last—until the young man adds, "But I'll tell you what surprises me most about this country. The bureaucracy is worse here than in Russia. I have had to fight to get my tourist visa, my working visa, my political asylum. I have never had so many papers in my life." Andreev gives me a what-is-to-be-done look.

Even his beloved wife, Natasha, lets him down on this score. Like the waiter, she is quick to complain about

America's "incredible red tape." But she appeases him by adding, "To be fair to our fellow Russians here, much of what appears to be arrogance comes from their isolation. In the Soviet Union, they fit into a system they did not want. Here they do not yet fit into a system they do want." She considers a second. "Yet all generalizations are wrong. Many, even most, are making their way here. And the next generation will all be Americans."

Of course, this is true. And when it happens, the newest Russian-Americans will do their best to slam the doors on the latest Russian immigrants. And so on, and so on. In another, and rougher, part of Brooklyn some years earlier, I spoke with a young Dominican woman named Anna about her immigrant experience. On the day we talked, a wake was held in a neighborhood funeral home for two young sisters, ages fifteen and four, who had died in a firebombing two nights before. The rumor was that their father was the target of a rival gang, but he was out when the bomb was tossed through his window. The father's gang showed up at the wake.

"I know that my own countrymen are responsible for a lot of the crime around here," Anna told me, "but they aren't the majority of us. The other Dominicans I work with are as afraid of the criminals as anyone else. They don't think of them as Dominicans, just criminals." She chuckled. "My mother says, 'You know what's wrong with this country? They let everybody in!'"

Andreev and I walk down to the ocean. I ask him what he sees. "Well," he says, "I see Far Rockaway over there and New Jersey over there, and over there a narrow passage leading to the open sea. But in my mind I can see Russia as well. And not only the gulags but my friends, whom I miss. Some of them were wonderful people. I belonged to them, in a way. But if I were there now, looking out across an ocean in this direction, I would still have my wild dreams."

Suddenly we come upon, nearly bump into, a young beautiful black woman wearing a demure blue suit and a pillbox hat. A convert to Judaism, she is handing out flyers for Sabbath candles, printed in Russian. "See?" says Andreev, sky-high again. "America!"

9

OUR LEADERS SAY
THE DARNDEST THINGS

*In which we watch the Detroit Tigers on radio when
we can, discover that Hawaii is in the Pacific, yet try
not to throw out the baby with the dishes*

* * *

Among the great joys of being an American is the opportunity to laugh at the people we elect to lead us. In fact, I sometimes suspect that we elect them for this purpose—not for being stupid, which they rarely are, but for saying imaginative and entertaining things. To me, a major letdown of the Clinton years was that, while he frequently behaved peculiarly, he did not speak peculiarly, and so failed to offer us the delights that most presidents do. I don't know why this is so, but nearly every president in my lifetime, and many other national leaders as well, has, at one time or another, sounded nuts.

Of course, America has not cornered the market on this form of entertainment. The term *faux pas* goes back at least to seventeenth-century France and originally referred to a woman's lapse of virtue—not that women make more false steps than the gender they step out with. In the 1960s, the slogan "Come Alive with Pepsi" flopped understandably in Germany, when it was translated "Come Alive out of the Grave with Pepsi." Elsewhere it was translated with more precision: "Pepsi Brings Your Ancestors Back from the Grave." In 1965, prior to a reception for Queen Elizabeth II outside Bonn, Germany's President Heinrich Lubke, attempting an English translation of *Gleich geht es los* (It will soon begin), told the queen "Equal goes it loose." The queen took the news well, but no better than the president of India, who was greeted at an airport in 1962 by Lubke, who, intending to ask "How are you?" instead said, "Who are you?" To which his guest answered responsibly, "I am the president of India."

American leaders make so many weird statements that we have come to regard such things as a normal part of government. Richard Nixon is thought of as a dark character, but he could be hilarious. There was the time of his first visit to the Great Wall of China. He turned to then Secretary of State William Rogers and said, "I think you would have to agree, Mr. Secretary, that this is a great wall." There was the time Mr. Nixon was on a state visit to attend President Pompidou's funeral. He arrived in Paris for the funeral and was immediately surrounded by film crews and reporters. He stepped out of his limousine, looked about, and said, "It's a great day for France."

I've long held the theory that Mr. Nixon was always meant to be a great comedian and only by a cruel turn of fate was he diverted from his proper destiny. I interviewed him a couple of times. At the first interview I put my tape recorder next to him. He looked at it and said, "Oh, that's one of those *new* tape recorders. They're so much better than the *old* tape recorders." I didn't know if he was joking. I did not laugh. I did not say, "Oh yes, Mr. President. They don't skip a minute." I did *not* say that.

I can only recall one memorable thing said by Gerald Ford, other than his famous statement in the 1976 presidential campaign that Poland was not under Soviet domination, which must have come as good news to Poland. Asked if he still followed baseball, Mr. Ford said, "I always watch the Detroit Tigers on radio when I can." I like the "when I can."

These are slips of the tongue, for which one may be

forgiven, though they frequently suggest what the speaker was really thinking. When the police broke up the demonstrations at the 1968 Democratic National Convention in Chicago, Mayor Daley put everybody at ease by explaining, "The policeman is not there to *create* disorder. He's there to *preserve* disorder." Concerned with events in Vietnam, Senator Kenneth Wherry from Nebraska made an impassioned speech in the Senate in which he referred throughout to "Indigo China." One has to be in the mood for such a speech. Even the deliberate-minded Woodrow Wilson said, "When enough people are out of work, unemployment results."

With Jimmy Carter, verbal mistakes may have had some deeper meaning, too. When Carter was in Warsaw, he wanted to express his warm feelings toward the people of Poland. This must be a presidential trait. Whatever it was he said came out translated in Polish as "I have lust in my heart for the people of Poland." Or variously "I want to make love to all the Polish people." For all his genuine good deeds since leaving office—and there have been many—Carter *in* office could seem kind of petty, bogged down in details, and he could get a little mean. Everyone knew that he thought Hubert Humphrey was a windbag. Still it came as a surprise, at the Democratic National Convention in 1980, when Carter referred to Hubert Horatio Humphrey as "Hubert Horatio Hornblower."

Ronald Reagan said some truly remarkable things. Returning from a trip to Latin America, he told us, "You'd be *surprised. They're all individual countries.*" "Sure, we made mistakes," he once said. "Point them out and we'll correct them. But, let's not throw the *baby* out with the *dishes.*" I'm not sure why, but my favorite thing Mr. Reagan ever said was after he had been listening to a half-hour lecture by the foreign minister of Lebanon, on Lebanese political factions. After the lecture, Reagan went up to the Lebanese foreign minister and said, "You know, your nose looks just like Danny Thomas's."

Former Vice President Dan Quayle said so many notable things, it is hard to choose one's favorite. Upon returning from a trip to Hawaii, he announced, "Hawaii has always been a very pivotal role in the Pacific. It is in the Pacific. It is part of the United States that is an island that is right here." Speaking about the toppling of the Berlin Wall, he conjectured, "I believe we are in an irreversible trend toward more freedom—but that could change." Quayle was an expert on national defense. He once explained, "Why wouldn't an enhanced deterrent, a more stable peace, a better prospect to denying the ones who enter conflict in the first place to have a reduction of offensive systems and an introduction to defensive capability." Exactly.

I miss George Bush the elder very much for the things he said—the man who praised Czechoslovakia's president, playwright Václav Havel, as "a hero who was in jail and dying, or living, whatever, for freedom." Or who described his own birthday party as "good cake, good card, and not bad." Or who offered his special analysis of the 1988 election: "It's no exaggeration to say that the undecideds could go one way or the other."

As for George W., he has offered many inspiring words since September 11, but he has also shown that he stands in the long tradition of American political speakers. Of his demonstrated presidential quality, he said, "A leadership is someone who brings people together." Of education: "Rarely is the question asked, 'Is our children learning?'" Of his reputation: "They misunderestimated me." Let us hope not.

10

WE ARE A BUNCH
OF LOSERS, OURSELVES

*In which we stand by the proposition that
losing isn't the only thing, it's everything*

☆ ☆ ☆

This is a time when we are intent on winning a just war, so we'll set aside some national attitudes that may seem to run counter to that purpose. But in peacetime we have as much affection for losing as for winning— more precisely for the character of the loser, who, under the proper circumstances, is endearing, even heroic. Losing in America is a very special thing, unlike losing in France, for example. Americans are not supposed to lose, and when we do, we tend to make something pleasant of the experience (nice guys finish last), maybe because we appreciate its usefulness in a culture that pretends to have no room for it.

But the lovable loser plays a big part in the American dream. It may be that only a country so accustomed to victories could afford to exalt the defeated, but we do it nonetheless. For a while there it appeared that the lovable loser had been dropped as a national figure, especially in recent years, when everyone was supposed to become a NASDAQ millionaire, and a loser really was a loser. But the figure is too valuable for the country's self-image to be done away with. Except for sports, nothing allows a clear-cut context for winning and losing, and the lovable loser—as long as he is on the side of the angels—rescues the country from its excesses, and thus represents an indispensable national trait.

The best example of this character I've seen lately is in the movie *Wonder Boys,* made faithfully from Michael Chabon's terrific novel. For one brief, miserable moment, Michael Douglas, the novelist-professor hero of the movie, has it all. His wife has left him. His girlfriend, the chancellor of his university, who is married to his department chairman, is pregnant with Douglas's child. His never-to-be-finished second novel has thickened to 2,611 pages, single-spaced. His gay editor is in town, hungry both for the new book and for Douglas's best student, a boy who gunned down the department chairman's dog when it bit Douglas on the leg. The wound has become infected. Douglas limps through the slush of a Pittsburgh winter, dressed in his former wife's pink chenille bathrobe. He hasn't shaved in three days. He drives around stoned, with the murdered dog in the trunk of the car, which he believes to be his but which was stolen from a man with a James Brown hairdo, who is out to get him.

A picture this lovely doesn't come along every day, but here it was—the lovable loser, the shimmering failure, the mess who for all his stumbles in the slush still strove for something honorable and was honored by the greater world in which he gloriously flopped.

On the same day that I saw *Wonder Boys,* I watched a different bunch of wonder boys (and women) strut their stuff on a TV special called *Summit in Silicon Valley.* ("Bunch" is wrong for the collective noun. An "exuberance"?) I watched an exuberance of high-tech billionaires sunning themselves in national adoration, bright models of achievement for every double-breasted hopeful yearning for a Lexus. No one mentioned lovable losers. The last shall be last. But these billionaires were not really America. They were the opposite numbers to the characters who practically defined American heroism, epic and tragic—Huck and Holden, Charlie Chaplin, Charlie Brown. Nearly all of Hemingway's heroes are defeated in *Winner Take Nothing* and in the novels. In *To Have and Have Not,* Harry Morgan had not. Bruce Springsteen sang about his "town full of losers." In *Rocky XXVIII,* our hero may finally knock out Adrian, but in his first fight in 1976, he lost splendidly.

In some ways, it is easier to be an American winner than a loser, which has certain definite requirements:

1. He has to serve as an affront to more purposeful lives. The most engaging character on the 1950s sitcom *My Little Margie* was the boyfriend, Freddie, whose job consisted of spending the day looking at construction sites.

2. His values have to be in the right place, but they also have to suggest that society's were in the wrong place. Muhammad Ali was stripped of his heavyweight title because he refused the draft to protest the Vietnam War. He wasn't a hero to everyone, but people recognized the gesture.

3. He has no use for money(!). A hero in his character, if not in his cause, was Robert E. Lee, who after his con-

siderable loss, was exhausted and without an income. An insurance company offered him $50,000 (easily a million dollars today) to use his name. Lee said, "I cannot consent to receive pay for services I do not render," and eventually accepted the presidency of small and impoverished Washington College, which became Washington and Lee after his death.

The main requirement for the lovable loser is that society must value him, must impute virtue to him for no other reason than he fails in a sincerely believed-in, preferably impeccable, cause. Before the 1980s, there was a public shame attached to too much success. That attitude was useless and irrational but also sweet-natured and not unhealthy. The underlying idea was that failure was something potentially good for you and for everyone, that rejection and loss were not only personally toughening but that losing was also a sign of high standards, or at least independent ones.

Even the makers of the Michael Douglas movie could not bear to leave their hero a lovable loser forever. At the end of the picture, there he is—clean-shaven, writing his new and tidy novel, his new wife and child emerging from his new car—all seen from a vast picture window in a new house so full of sunlight it makes one long for slush.

Yet it is the slob who tramps around in his wife's pink bathrobe whom we honor and cherish—the one who beats the system by being beaten by the system. Behold Rodney Dangerfield, who claimed to have received a publishers sweepstakes letter that read "You may already be a loser." Rodney also said that when he enters an elevator, the operator asks, "Down?" Looks like up to me.

11

OUR HOUSE IS A
VERY VERY VERY FINE HOUSE

In which we look at the Constitution as if
we lived there. Who chose those drapes?

✶ ✶ ✶

Practically everything good and great about America
stems from the Constitution. The beauty of the document is that it does all the things a written constitution
is supposed to do—set up a political and electoral system, identify permissions and prohibitions, create a
framework for the economy, and so forth—but it also
provides an attitude, a guidebook for living as an American. Its authors could not have produced so durable a
piece of work without a vision of the person to whom
the laws and stipulations were directed. Look at the
words. Read them not as rules of the game but as the in-
terior ruminations of a character, a hero, who in some

strange conflicted combination of exultation and self-restraint has, for over two hundred years, found a way to conduct a life.

The house he occupies is as strange as he is, at once balanced and shaky, like a house of cards. The basic text of the Constitution is the main building, a symmetrical eighteenth-century structure grounded in the Enlightenment's principles of reason, optimism, order, and a wariness of emotion and passion. The Constitution's architects, all fundamentally British Enlightenment minds, sought to build a home that Americans could live in without toppling it by placing their impulses above their rationality. To these men, who grew up on Swift, Hume, Locke, and Pope, stability and moderation were not only practical measures but signs of morality. To put it brutally, the framers created these counterweights because they didn't really trust us.

Ben Franklin, when he wrote of striving for moral perfection in the *Autobiography*, said that he originally set his ambitions in the light of an already God-perfected world. "Whatever is, is right," he quoted John Dryden; Pope used precisely the same line in "An Essay on Man." Washington, whose presence hovered over the Constitutional Convention like a muse, also advocated moderation: "We [Americans] are apt to run from one extreme to another," he wrote John Jay in 1786. As for Madison, the Constitution's principal and most elegant-minded architect, his views were straight Enlightenment dogma. "Why has government been instituted at all?" he asked. "Because the passions of men will not conform to the dictates of reason and justice, without constraint." Again: "If men were angels, no government would be necessary"—as much a judgment of angels as of people.

The collective wisdom behind all such statements envisions human nature as existing in and requiring for its survival the most delicate array of balances between religion and science, reason and emotion, democracy and aristocracy, the individual and the group, self-interest and general welfare; that is, all the balances that found their way into the Constitution's basic text. On the whole, that original, unamended text is a model Enlightenment tract, carefully checking and balancing as if in imitation of the moderate universe in which eighteenth-century Europe trusted. One of the framers, John Dickinson, even saw the proposed relationship between the states and the federal government as an analogue to

Newtonian physics, and why not? Whatever is, is right. If the "man" Pope considered in his "Essay" needed a body of laws, the American Constitution would do just fine.

The trouble with that original body of laws, as Henry May concluded in his study *The Enlightenment in America,* was that it reflected "all the virtues of the Moderate Enlightenment, and also one of its faults: the belief that everything can be settled by compromise." In other words, the basic Constitution was *too* balanced, and thus logically flawed. What moderate compromises are available when a nation seeks to retain the institution of slavery? The answer to the Constitution's excessive symmetry was the Bill of Rights, which did not overturn the basic document but represented a risky extension into the realms of individual freedom that many of the framers thought dangerous. So here was the Enlightenment house with an ell attached, and a riddle: Yes, the main structure was perfect, and, yes, it needed continuous work. Very cute.

What sort of person would live in such a house? An eighteenth-century person, in fact, but one whose mind spanned the entire century, adding the late-eighteenth-century expansiveness—the wild-and-crazy guyness—of Blake and Wordsworth to the wary constraints of Pope.

The century that began in the Age of Reason ended in the Age of Romanticism, and the Constitution accommodated that raucous transition. If the basic text is an Enlightenment document, the Bill of Rights is an homage to Romantic thought, challenging not so much the specifics of the basic Constitution but rather its earnest sense of permanence. Amendments did not promise answers to sentimental wishes, but they did build in rooms for restlessness. Amendments promised more, and "more" is a Romantic idea. The person who lived in the Constitution was born in the last century that equally prized both modesty and fantasy, and he shuttled naturally between the poles.

After 215 years he has changed dramatically, from an eighteenth-century Englishman to a modern African-American, Asian, Latino. His clothes are more fun, and his lingo jazzier. But in terms of basic human nature, he remains as he was when the country began. In two centuries his equilibrium has been tested constantly in a history that includes a secession of half the country, two world wars, Prohibition, a civil rights movement, a war over abortion, burgeoning fundamentalism, and a thousand exigencies that the Constitution's framers could not have possibly foreseen. Yet, amazingly, they could foresee this character at the center of their work: the basic Enlightenment man with a capacity for explosions and a touch of the poet. Much like themselves, he was capable of sitting still as a stone and of changing on a dime.

That he has survived these 215 years seems due largely to the Constitution's roominess, which has given him space to shift the furniture without destroying the house. The genius of the Constitution is that it offers its resident a perpetual challenge to find his own equilibrium within the structure. Miraculously, to date he has managed to do that, as if he were conscious of the fact that the Constitution reflects his nature, mirrors his competing tendencies to squat adamantly and lurch suddenly. In a way, he continually rediscovers himself in that house, a brand-new American for every decade of problems.

Yet if the Constitution allows this character to create himself, the character also creates the Constitution, for he existed before it was conceived, and it was built to suit his mind. It's astonishing that that mind has endured, given its obvious weaknesses and failings. Perhaps its endurance has something to do with the fact that it runs on a fundamentally generous impulse, that it is the mind of a country that saw itself from the start as an institution

of welcome, seeking doggedly to make good on a promise to provide a free, just home. That generous impulse is
equally stabilizing and liberating, like the document that
promotes it. Who lives in the Constitution? Look again.
You handsome devil.

12

We Can Live with It

*In which such problematic issues as abortion,
affirmative action, war, privacy, and capital
punishment are settled to everyone's satisfaction*

* * *

For a people who walk around cocksure of their one
favorite political party, football team, fast-food restaurant, and brand of beer, we are remarkably capable of living with compromising, complicated, and incompatible
ideas. Contradiction in American thought is part of the
deal. The country actually functions better in a conflicted state of mind than it does when everything is
clean and tidy. We are by now used to a certain degree of
conflict in every major problem of national life. Very few
people who oppose capital punishment do not at one
point of their lives think "kill him" when they learn of an

especially vicious murderer. People who oppose affirmative action in the workplace often do not oppose it in the context of school admissions, where many different kinds of quotas are quietly filled and acknowledged.

The exceptions may prove the rule in such areas, but as in the feeling that certain killers ought to be put to death, it is by the exceptional circumstances that one knows the entirety of one's true mind. Chances are that the more significant the problem, the less adamantly it will be considered by honest thinkers. For such honest thinkers there will always be the instructive presence of doubt, which, in a way, provides the individual citizen's balance of power.

The idea of living with conflict does not mean mere sufferance. Neither individuals nor the country as a whole would be able to succeed by living with conflict if all it meant was grinning and bearing unbearable circumstances. We're not good grinners and bearers by nature. But for us living with conflict means an acknowledgment of apparently incompatible elements within an acceptable system—Fitzgerald's dictum about one's being able to function while holding contrary thoughts played out on a national stage. We are for both federal assistance and states' autonomy; we are for both the First Amendment and normal standards of propriety; we are for both the rights of privacy and the needs of public health; and so forth. Our most productive thinking usually contains a clear inner confession of mixed feelings; our least productive, a nebulous irritation resulting from a refusal to come to terms with disturbing and patently irreconcilable ideas.

Consider just a few of the major contradictions we live with. For starters, take abortion. That issue, which threatened to toss us into civil war only a decade ago, has calmed down to a whisper, in part because, in the interests of compromise, there was a little chipping away at *Roe* v. *Wade* in the June 1992 Supreme Court decision in *Casey* v. *Planned Parenthood* in Pennsylvania (women must be informed of alternatives to abortion and unmarried girls under eighteen must get parental consent); and in greater part because warring groups have come to their senses, and to common ground, by agreeing that the best formula for the country to adopt is "permit-but-discourage." That's really what we always wanted anyway. In the 1970s (thanks to us liberals, I'm sorry to say), abortion was allowed to appear solely as a political issue.

In fact, it was mainly a private moral and emotional issue, and we've come to see that. Think: fifteen years ago, an explosive demonstration over abortion was a nightly news regular. When was the last time you heard a peep about it?

Yet, *Roe* remains intact. Women continue to have abortions legally, when they need them. The things to keep an eye on are medical schools that no longer teach abortion, and other impediments to abortion such as forcing women to travel too far to get one. But, as long as women's rights are preserved, and the painful choice they make is also acknowledged, the country will deal with it. What's interesting about our being able to live with this matter is that it goes to the heart of American thought. The invention of abortion, like other instruments of American optimism, cuts both ways. One may praise the procedure as something that allows women to realize full control over their invented selves. Or one may damn the procedure as one that destroys forever the possibility of a new life inventing itself. As with all else pertaining to this issue, one's moral position depends on the direction in which one is looking. Yet both points of view are inspired by optimism, and both see life in America as the best of choices.

Or take our class system. We are as mired in a class system as any European culture, the difference being that Europe built its classes out of birthright, and we built ours out of cash. Yet we don't talk about it, because the very idea of class threatens the ideal of equality. So, very quietly, we have simply evolved into a multiplicity of classes, including the information class created by the emerging technologies. The way America has structured itself, we live surrounded only by people who live as we do. Homes in like neighborhoods cost the same; schools are alike; clothing and manners are similar; people socialize with their economic peers. We live cocooned with members of our own class, yet we are so eager to hide this fact from one another, that most of us haven't the slightest notion of what class we belong to.

So we don't mention it. We remain extremely uncomfortable with our class system, and that's that. Our embarrassment about this business is probably good for us, and it rescues us from the hatreds and social misdemeanors that usually attend class distinctions. But we are wise to live with it because there is nothing we can do about it. Open talk about our hypocrisy would undoubtedly hurl us into fistfights. We're not as dumb as we look.

Then there's war. We are both extremely reluctant to get into a war and exceedingly effective when we do. We didn't raise our country to be a soldier. As a people, we have no taste for war. We resist it—sometimes a little too long. The gangsters who attacked us on September 11 thought we were too soft and complacent to fight back. How little they know us. When it comes to war, we simply want to win and get out as soon as possible. At the start of World War II, we ranked twenty-seventh in armaments among the nations of the world. By the war's end—thanks to Rosie and her fellow riveters—we were number one, with second place nowhere in sight. But we only got in to crush other gangsters and get it over with. You may feel differently about the Bomb than I do (I think it was a damned necessity), but that, too, was a way of ending a war and saving American lives.

Frankly, to my mind, our main danger in our ability to live with contradictory impulses in war is that it will encourage us to conclude the current mission against terrorism before the mission is complete. We got out of Iraq too soon, too. On the whole, it is better to err on the side of peace and safety—as long as we know where they lie. In any case, for a country as powerful as ours to be able to live with antipodal attitudes toward fighting is a saving grace.

To give ourselves an idea of just how far we will go with this national juggling act, we even—can I spit this out?—think in polar ways about lawyers. We rail against the litigious society and against the particular ambulance-chaser who is making life hell for us, but when we're in most kinds of trouble, who're we gonna call? We hate lawyers and we love laws, or more generally, what we call the rule of law. It is no small matter to live in a country that runs according to laws. Try taking a look at places like Cambodia, Beirut, Sudan, and Rwanda, as I have, and the point is made. We show our divided minds on this subject by relishing lawyer jokes, while glomming on to cultural representations of the law as well: *Court TV, Law & Order,* even *Ally McBeal.* As was said in the 1948 English movie *The Winslow Boy,* about a court case: "Let right be done." We believe that it will be, and we trust lawyers with our lives.

Oh, all right. A lawyer, a Hindu, and a rabbi are driving along when their car breaks down. They approach a farmhouse. The farmer says that he has room for two of them to spend the night in the house, but that one has to stay in the barn with the pig and the cow. The Hindu volunteers first, but a few minutes later there's a knock on the farmer's door. The Hindu says he can't sleep with the pig and the cow. The rabbi goes next, but he, too, returns with the same complaint. Finally, the lawyer goes out. A few moments later, there's a knock at the door. It's the pig and the cow. Happy now?

13

WE'D RATHER NOT BE RICH

*In which it is established that the rich are
different from you and me—they're funnier*

✳ ✳ ✳

We have always been divided in our reactions to the rich; we laugh at them, and we want to be them. Laughing is easier. At the turn of the nineteenth century, and progressing into the twentieth, there was a ceaseless vaudeville show consisting of millionaires' excesses. Cornelius Vanderbilt set up a fifty-eight-room mansion on Fifth Avenue with a ballroom that was a replica of Versailles. Hearst's San Simeon, situated on a plot of land half the size of Rhode Island, had its own airfield, its own train, thirty-five limousines, and the largest private zoo in the world, not counting where the people were kept. "Every time Willie feels badly," said Hearst's mother, "he goes out and buys something." Potter Palmer, the

Chicago hotel and store owner, draped his wife in so many diamonds that the woman could not stand upright. Diamond Jim Brady showed his affection for actress Lillian Russell by buying her a diamond-and-gold bicycle. "Mount some diamonds on the handlebars," he told the guy who made it for him, "for class."

What pleasure movies in the Depression years took in showing the idiot rich at play—as in the wonderful *My Man Godfrey,* which begins with a bunch of spoiled, over-age brats on a scavenger hunt. A horde of dim-witted playboys and playgirls comb the city in search of a forgotten man—a hobo, who will be the prize quarry in the hunt.

WILLIAM POWELL: Do you mind telling me just what a scavenger hunt is?

CAROLE LOMBARD: Well, a scavenger hunt is exactly like a treasure hunt, except in a treasure hunt, you try to find something you want, and in a scavenger hunt, you try to find something that nobody wants.

POWELL: Like a forgotten man.

LOMBARD: That's right. And the one that wins gets a prize, only there really isn't a prize. It's just the honor of winning, because all the money goes to charity, that is, if there's any money left over, but there never is.

This sort of nonsense used to be more amusing than it has been lately because lots of formerly ordinary people are able to afford the accoutrements of the rich. Why laugh at them when you can join 'em? For their part, the rich are cannier about public relations than they used to be. Bill Gates buys up all the world's Gutenberg Bibles (ridiculous) while he sets up a huge philanthropic foundation (smart).

Still, we have our share of billionaire entertainers. *Ocean Navigator* magazine reports that poor Jim Clark, a cofounder of Netscape, was unsatisfied with his 155-foot sailing yacht, *Hyperion,* and so, before the boat was even launched, ordered up a bigger boat, a 292-foot schooner named *Athena.* Clark complained that the 155-foot job was simply too small for his needs. *Athena* may turn out to be insufficient as well. Clark is already thinking of a boat large enough for a helicopter. "I have a policy," he said, "that I get to spend as much on myself as I give away." Larry Ellison, the public-minded billionaire chairman of Oracle, has just bought a $10-million yacht with a basketball court. For the rich, size matters. One of these yachts, says *Power and Motor Yacht* magazine editor Diane Byrne, uses over seven hundred tons of marble in its Turkish bath and has a staircase like the *Titanic*—quite a recommendation.

As for the rest of us, we continue to covet riches, but always with the traditional endearing mixture of impulses. The successful TV show, *Who Wants to Be a Millionaire?*, gets its name from an old song in which the answer to that question is "I don't." We are ashamed about having money in the abstract because the idea conjures up cultural guilt feelings. We are ashamed of talking about our own money, though we don't mind talking about someone else's.

All this also affects our attitude toward the poor, whom we are willing, even eager, to help—personally or by way of the government—but whom we would still rather not mention. In the world of bigots, one will hear ethnic and racial insults much more often than a word of disapproval about the poor. In my lifetime, I don't believe that I have ever heard someone put down because he has little or no money, and that is probably because we take money so seriously. It is to us as sex was to the Victorians—habitual and unmentionable.

"Sorry, son, I can't tell you how much Daddy makes." "Sure, we're getting divorced, but money won't be an issue." "It's not about the money." And on and on. When the stock market dives we call our reaction a "panic" because the damn thing is so emotional, because money is the stuff of our self-worth, safety, beauty. And (sorry) it will, or can, buy you love. As a young man, I measured my fiscal substantiality by whether or not I could afford the ten-pack of razor blades or the five. I remember blowing up in a rage at the man at the cleaners, who, against my instructions, cleaned a pair of my pants (five dollars) instead of pressing them (two dollars).

Why is it that no great American novel has ever been written about business, a possible exception being William Dean Howell's *A Modern Instance*? Because business is about money (acquisition or loss), and money is what we do most and best. Even when Hollywood deals with business transactions, it portrays money purely as an emotional weapon. No one has ever understood the wheelings and dirty dealings in the movie *Wall Street*. The point of the movie was to have Michael Douglas utter the forbidden words "Greed is good"—possibly the worst thing ever said in a movie made in the land of the equals—because (gulp) it rang true.

There is no way out of our conflict of impulses as long as human capabilities and plain good luck are distributed unfairly. But you have to love a country that refuses to knuckle under to the facts. America may be money crazy, but in principle we deplore it. And out of that principle comes every national effort, however sporadic, to raise the lot of the poor, the disadvantaged, the out-of-work.

Besides, the rich still behave badly enough to provide some entertainment. In the Hamptons, the wealthy publicist Lizzie Grubman backed her car into a crowd she designated as "white trash." Some years ago, Wall Street's Saul Steinberg threw himself a million-dollar birthday party. If we run out of amusing Americans, we can always refer to Aristotle Onassis, who wanted to buy the island of Ithaca because it had been the home of Odysseus; or the Maharajah of Baroda, who gave his elephant diamond earrings worth $125,000 (she looked fabulous); or good old Nero, who had a 150-foot statue of himself put up in his palace. He looked it over and said, "At last I am beginning to live like a human being."

14

WE SHAME MONSTERS

*In which the free exercise of public opinion forces two big,
bad wolves to see the light*

★ ★ ★

The National Rifle Association did something odd
not long ago, even by its standards. Responding to the
Million Mom March in Washington for gun control,
the NRA presented television and newspaper ads in
which its president, Charlton Heston, and an "NRA
mom" announced a new challenge program. "We're putting up the first $1 million to put gun-safety education in
every classroom," said Heston. The NRA mom added,
"That's a million NRA moms challenging a million
more moms just like you."

I'm not sure what an NRA mom is, though one
wonders what she puts in the kids' lunchboxes. But I
know an impressive "outreach" initiative when I see one.

The Philip Morris Co. has been engaging in similar efforts for the past year or so. The-tobacco-and-so-much-more company has new ads proclaiming its support of the "We Card" program to prevent children from buying cigarettes. In the ad, a bunch of kids dressed for a prom attempt to buy smokes from a kindly yet firm store owner, who tells us that belonging to the "We Card" program makes it easier for him to turn down the kids. There is a lacuna in logic here, but the point, apparently, is that Philip Morris opposes killing anyone until he reaches majority.

Redemption through good works, or the effort to achieve it, is almost always a heartening sight even when one knows that for the NRA and Philip Morris, redemption is good for business. Advertising, as we have learned from long experience, is an invention of alchemy. The NRA and Philip Morris fervently hope that if they continue to fill TV screens and papers with their exciting promotions, it will not be long before our eagerly malleable subconsciouses associate both organizations with the polar opposite of what they really do for a living.

That said, these redemptive activities on the part of certain businesses and interest groups do represent bona fide good deeds. Philip Morris, in fact, is nearly as diversified in civic work as it is in its profit centers. It has launched a $100-million-a-year campaign to reshape its image by backing the environment, the arts, and summer camps for children with HIV or AIDS. Without Philip Morris, many of the best arts programs in the country would be hanging by a thread.

The interesting thing about these charitable thrusts is not that they are transparently insincere (they might be or not), but rather that they occurred at all. In what other country could two immensely rich special interests, with billions of dollars at their disposal, and billions to lose in the transactions, be made to acknowledge the harm they do without being forced to cease doing the harm? Had Philip Morris and the NRA not heard a growing cry of shame from the public—whether or not that outcry was fortified by laws or law suits—they never would have felt compelled to be socially concerned and to make amends. But the public did cry out so forcefully and definitely that two giants of destructive industry understood that at least they had to appear to clean up their acts.

And yet the public opinion that created their redemptive urges is almost untraceable. To be sure, there are opinion polls that show a lot of people opposed to guns and cigarettes. But it is hard to imagine the gun manufacturers or tobacco executives sitting at the breakfast table, reading opinion polls and deciding to act responsibly. Public opinion in this great republic operates more subtly and mysteriously than that—and, I think, more personally. Before the last decade or so, the people who ran these two industries remained anonymous. Nothing required them to show their faces in public. Recently, however, they have had to defend themselves on television again and again. And that is because there is always some horrendous event—a mass shooting, a person dying of lung cancer—that hauls them out of their holes. No darker moment ever befell the tobacco industry than when the company heads sat in a row before Congress and us and swore up and down that smoking was not addictive.

Once exposed in that way, the basic indecencies of their enterprises are also exposed. First they face the nation; then they have to walk among other citizens, among their own families, who recognize them and begin to shun them. Shunning is an old Puritan practice, but it works in every era in a democracy, and while it may be barbaric if applied to the wearer of a scarlet A, it is quite useful when directed at those who harm the rest of us.

For my suspicious self, I do not believe that either Philip Morris or the NRA would have lifted a finger to help artists or children if they did not perceive a general disapproval of their main activities. Perhaps they secretly disapproved themselves. No matter. The force of shame freely exercised turned two monsters into demi-monsters, which gets us half way home. Of course, the other half depends on what people want for themselves, which is where public humiliation can bite us in the ass. If we really want to put these industries out of their primary businesses, we have to shame ourselves into not buying what they're selling. Monsters lurk everywhere in the lovable country.

15

STILL HISTORICAL AFTER
ALL THESE YEARS

*In which we dive into the past, where we
splash about quite happily, thanks*

☆ ☆ ☆

There comes a terrible moment to many souls,"
George Eliot wrote in *Daniel Deronda,* "when the great
movements of the world, the larger destinies of mankind, which have lain aloof in newspapers and other
neglected reading, enter like an earthquake into their
lives." Tell me about it. But something more fundamental and revealing happened after September 11 as well.
For many years—twelve since the toppling of the Berlin
Wall and the Soviet threat; twenty-seven since Water-
gate, depending on how you're counting—the country
was living outside history. By this I mean living not only
with little regard for the larger destinies of mankind but

also outside the stories, lessons, and issues that locate us within significant patterns of human thought. Now a group of savage zealots has flung us back into history, where we feel very much at home.

But nobody ever says that. The conventional wisdom about America and the past is that we hate the tense, are always striding forward (implied, blindly), and when the best of us dreamers yearn to make some progress, we are dragged relentlessly back. America is the original original country. We came into being when the burden of the past had already grown too heavy for eighteenth-century Europe, so it has always been assumed that the country is uncomfortable with history. Actually, we are crazy about it, tend to use it well, and only recently abandoned it, for which we paid a price.

Shortly after we were attacked, observers lamented that had the country only been more alert to world conditions (Islam, Afghanistan, international terrorism) and less enthralled with surface ephemera (O. J., Elian Gonzalez, Monica, Gary Condit), we might have avoided our current troubles. This was to imply that a few canny geopolitical decisions here and there would be all it would have taken to make the country safe and snug.

But history demands that one be aware of the deeper

world as well as the wider. For the period in question, America was hydroplaning on the present, creating and devouring a culture consisting of nonsense. The so-called intellectual life became deconstructionist game-playing, politics became claptrap, "globalization" became internationalism for shoppers. Our superpowerhood fed feelings of omnipotence and self-righteousness, which in turn created a false sense of immunity. We were told that the nation was a "city on a hill." On September 11, airplanes crashed into two cities on a hill.

What went unacknowledged was that everyone occupies a position in the great stream of events and ideas, even in a time of rampant vapidity; and to forget that was to lose one's bearings, along with one's soul. *Moby Dick* begins with Ishmael seeing his voyage as an interlude squeezed between more significant events, which he presents as newspaper headlines (you'll smile at his examples):

Grand Contested Election for the Presidency
  Of the United States
Whaling Voyage by One Ishmael
Bloody Battle in Affghanistan [sic]

Had he not believed that every individual belongs to history, his story would not have been worth telling.

Even during this period, we never abandoned the past entirely. While we were stepping away from history on one level, we were still clinging to it on another. The new memorials erected in this country indicate not only a passion for the past, but also for its complexities. Places like the Manzanar National Historical Site in the California desert, where an internment camp for Japanese-Americans was located in World War II, and the forty-two sites dedicated to the bloody history of the civil rights movement indicate that the country has been as interested in the shadows of its history as in the light. Not long ago local residents wanted to tear down Columbine High School. Now they are planning to create a plaza and memorialize the library where the killings occurred. The Vietnam Veterans Memorial and the United States Holocaust Memorial in Washington consecrate ordinary people and offer places where ordinary people can reach personal understandings.

The reason that history is central to us is that it requires every life to see itself as part of every other life. The history one feels these days is not only national and political but also the history of grief, unity, companionship; the history of fear, invasion, and sacrifice. One looks to the history of Britain during the Blitz, or to the history of the Jews who held history dear because it depended on time without place. All the past stories that apply to whatever one experiences these days are suddenly unearthed, and we are rushed back into the story of the entire species, in every dimension, the crucible of all of history's messages, even if those messages are sometimes scrambled.

On everyone's back is everyone else, which evokes the most important kind of history America has always tried to connect with: the history of doing the right thing. If we have sometimes been the country of very bad deeds, we have also been the country of moral corrections. Compare the treatment of the Japanese after Pearl Harbor to the treatment of Muslims since September 11. In spite of some disastrous international blunders, the country has still done more to benefit the rest of the world than any in history. We may be the only country ever interested in benefiting the rest of the world. We went into Bosnia for no other purpose than doing the right thing—something Muslim states might recall when railing against the Great Satan.

Of all the American characteristics cast off in recent years, the most essential was that of searching for a more ethical existence. America had pretty much cornered the market on that search, and when it was abandoned, the country lost its way. History is reorienting, but it does more than that. It enhances a life by extending it beyond its temporal limits. We go back to discover what we were, which teaches us what we are, and what we ought to be.

16

WE DON'T STOP THE PRESSES

*In which all the complex arguments and characteristics
that involve freedom of the press—including the crude
invasions of privacy that reporters engage in, the frequent
inaccuracy of the news, its liberal bias, its self-referential
tendencies, its seeking of bad news rather than good, its
substitution of gossip for fact, its predisposition for the
licentious and scatological, and its general nastiness,
incompetence, and unfairness—are reduced
to a single question:*

* * *

What's not to love?

17

WE WON'T BE
HORNSWOGGLED

In which the astonishingly good sense of most of the
people most of the time makes most of the media look silly

☆ ☆ ☆

It is equally amazing and gratifying to see how sensible the American people can be if given enough time and information—especially since we also go through so many spasms of idiocy. Afflicted with a sort of national ADD, we take up fads at the drop of a streaking pet rock. And we get taken in from time to time by very dangerous snake-oil salesmen, like Joe McCarthy, who turned fads into nightmares. But, on the whole, we will not be buffaloed, hoodwinked, bamboozled, or—to continue the mystifying Gabby Hayes cowboy lingo—hornswoggled. Lincoln was right. And the reason you can't fool all of us consistently has to do with the way the free mind works.

We say casually that people were born to be free, but we do not always ask why, and the answer, among others—that freedom makes us creative, expansive, scared, and so forth—is that it also makes us smarter. By that I don't mean that if we're allowed to read and study anything we wish, we'll have more brain power; that's a given. I mean that the mind, offered the opportunity to simply observe and ruminate, will eventually—sometimes after a long and bumpy flight—land on the truth.

Think back to the Clinton/Monica impeachment business that now, particularly after September 11, seems so distant and small change. Yet only a couple of years ago it was the talk of every town. The talk started in the press, which is where scandalous talk usually starts. Since, at the time, there was no competing story to fill the vacuum (which, by the way, is how other stories, such as Elian Gonzalez and Gary Condit come to be inflated to the size of Thanksgiving Day balloons), the Clinton story strode the nation like a Colossus. (There were a couple of other stories in progress during the time, such as the al-Qaeda group's saber rattling, which went unreported.) Nonetheless, in the apparent media doldrums, Clinton's weird antics grew from something merely distasteful, albeit *very* distasteful, to the story of a national calamity.

Naturally, Republican congressmen and senators became the story's most avid fans. And together with the press (for once), though not in conspiracy, they thought they could and should bring down a president. They had caught him with his pants down—or open—after all, and they had caught him, as did we, in a lie akin to perjury. Ergo: the president must go.

And yet, while others were giving Clinton the bum's rush, the reputedly sloggy, sleepy, laid-back, barely sentient American people were privately and quietly arriving at a different conclusion. No one approved of Clinton's behavior, much less condoned the flouting of the law. But we also did not like where the media and Clinton's political enemies were leading us. We clearly demonstrated that in opinion polls and in the midterm elections by not turning the Democrats out. When push finally came to call the question of shove, Clinton was not impeached. Why? Because we could tell a high crime from a misdemeanor (or an embarrassed demeanor). And it was damn lucky that we could.

Republican pols were not generally pleased with the outcome of the Clinton story, but the press, to its belated credit, did eventually pick up on the fact that most of us people had our heads on straight. In a way, we rewrote the Clinton story because, like good editors, we saw where that story was going to come out, and we simply rejected that particular ending. We found it implausible, unpersuasive. So we got the ending we wanted—immediately after which, you'll remember, the story crept away like Carl Sandburg's fog on little cat's feet. Speaking of Sandburg, the people yes.

You can tell a great deal about the significance of a story by the presence or absence of reverberations, and this one had none. The nice thing is that it was the people who noticed. We contradicted everything we were being told to do and ignored the Sturm and the Drang. It may not always be thus, but one reason for loving this place is that the basic ground of the free mind is bedrock good sense, and the test of our use of the free mind is often to find that solid ground. That's where freedom's own story usually leads, which is where we live almost happily ever after.

18

WHEN LEFT TO OUR OWN DEVICES, WE BEGIN TO BEHAVE PRETTY WELL

In which the hypothesis is offered that Americans are growing kinder with one another and may be experiencing evolutionary improvement

✳ ✳ ✳

Already pushing fast from the south, the wind must have tripled its power after mounting the hill, then it charged straight at the glass and brick wall of the East Coldenham Elementary School cafeteria. Between the hill and the wall the land lies flat as a dish, so there was nothing to break the momentum. When the sky went dark, some of the 120 kids eating in the cafeteria jumped up from their seats to stare bug-eyed at the wind beating on the glass. It was then that the wall, glass and brick together, exploded on top of them. Seven children, second and third graders, were crushed to death at once. Two more died in the hospital.

For a few days after November 16, 1989, the disaster made national news, then it shrank back to its original location in the middle Hudson River Valley region of New York State. It was the sort of story one did not want to hear, for once heard, it roots in the memory like something personal, a curse waiting for you. The parents of those children—how did they survive that day? How does anyone survive such a day? The entire population of the area, wrapped in wailing and grief, would have been forgiven for wishing to dig a crater and bury themselves beside the children in the earth.

Yet on a blank, gray morning in early December, three weeks after the disaster, everything looked normal and routine. It was not that the people had forgotten what had happened. To the contrary: In the towns surrounding the school, American flags flapped at half-mast, and there were notes of sympathy crayoned in the windows of the houses. At the fire station, which responded immediately when the wall blew down, a sign read THANKS TO ALL FOR HELPING COLDENHAM COPE. MAY GOD BLESS YOU. Plywood filled the space of the former wall. In blue spray paint someone had written:

RIP THOSE ~~YOU~~, ~~HOW~~ DIED—the writer having crossed out the YOU and the HOW in an unsuccessful search for WHO. Pinned to the makeshift wall were cloth flowers and stuffed animals—a skunk, a blue elephant in yellow sunglasses, a white bear in a T-shirt reading MAKE THE DISTANCE BEARABLE . . . CALL!

What the people of the region were doing, it seems to me, was using their sympathy for one another in order to survive. This is a growing practice in the country, especially in the past thirty or forty years. Americans these days are not only behaving better in groups than we do as individuals; we are behaving better in groups than we ever did. Historically, we are not that long removed from the lynch mobs (north and south), from phalanxes of enraged white parents spitting on black schoolchildren, from black and Latino mobs in the cities killing and looting, and other too-familiar memories. But we haven't seen such things in quite a while. A sign of evolutionary improvement is when people behave a bit better in groups. Are we evolving? Whatever happened to the bad old American mob?

I saw a situation similar to East Coldenham in East Moriches on Long Island. This was the summer of 2000, when TWA Flight 800 went down off Moriches Bay in the Atlantic on its way to Paris. As soon as the plane hit the water, dozens of folks who happened to be out fishing on a summer evening directed their boats toward the crash site. They told me afterward that they went out in hopes of finding people still alive. All they found was the detritus of the wreckage and body parts. One guy, who had not been able to sleep for thirty-six hours, told me "I never saw a dead person before, and now this. I prayed: Please don't let me find a kid. Then I found a kid."

East Moriches was in mourning for weeks, months, after the crash, in sympathy with strangers. The feeling—not unlike the feeling for those lost on September 11—extended way beyond one town. In my village of Quogue, ten miles to the east, people walked the beaches for many days after the crash, in a kind of civic funeral procession. They picked up dolls and eyeglasses that had been washed ashore and put them in collection boxes set out by the Coast Guard. For a long while, they did not swim in the ocean, as a sign of respect for the dead. When they passed one another on the beach, they nodded simply in gestures of recognition.

An incident in Billings, Montana, in the mid-1990s is now well-known, but is worth recalling as well. In the Christmas-Hanukkah season, members of the Ku Klux

Klan and other subhumans invaded the town of eighty thousand which, within its mainly white population, held a few hundred African-Americans, the same number of American Indians, and still fewer Latinos and Jews. The subhumans pushed down headstones in the Jewish cemetery, harassed a seventy-six-year-old black minister in his church, scrawled swastikas on the walls of the house of an American Indian woman, then threw a cinder block through a child's window because they saw a menorah in it.

The ministers of the town—having had a bellyful— got together. One of them recalled the useful-if-false story about the King of Denmark who, when ordered by the Nazis to make the Danish Jews wear yellow stars, wore one himself. So did many of his countrymen, who suggested symbolically that everyone in Denmark was Jewish. The *Billings Gazette* printed a full-page picture of a menorah which ten thousand Billings citizens clipped and taped in their windows. Then, everyone in Billings was an African-American, an Indian, and a Jew.

In a small Texas town a few years ago, a couple of other subhumans tied a black man to the back of their truck and dragged him to death. The town—mayor, civic leaders, ordinary citizens—rose up and spoke out in moral outrage against them. One might say, so what? But forty years ago—no matter how they might have condemned the murder privately—those people would not have said a word.

I tend to think of these group responses—and there are many more instances—as works of the imagination, the mind attaching itself to the hardships or the sufferings of others. They may be seen as forecasts of the way the country as a whole behaved after September 11—not only in its acts of sympathy, but also in the refusal to harass Muslims or to accept infringements of civil liberties, among other signs of improved group conduct. There are several possible reasons for these improvements over the years, ranging from the enactment of laws, to the exposures of TV news, to historians who have unearthed such national monstrosities as picture postcards of lynchings from as recently as 1960, showing smiling, formally dressed people in groups enjoying picnics as African-Americans were burned at the stake. But the principal reason, I think, is traced to a basic and decent sense of connectedness. For all our ardent diversities, for all our individual lurches, we still think of ourselves as one people—edgy, wary, competitive, yet related.

All the flags, the signs, the stuffed animals, and flowers in East Coldenham were works of the imagination. By such signals, the people of the region were telling one another that they sympathized—not casually or fleetingly, but deeply and permanently—like outsiders who recognize in their own circumstances the same susceptibility to sudden death. If faith is the imagination's most sublime form, human sympathy is its most precious. Around the East Coldenham school existed a community of suffering as well as a community of help.

So we had the memorial to the bombing victims in Oklahoma City. The people of the city chose the design of the memorial, which consisted of rows of chairs arranged where the victims had been working, to make the point that the dead were ordinary fellow citizens. So the Vietnam Memorial wall was erected that we could run our fingers over the names of our dead countrymen. So a memorial will be created for September 11, and, whatever it is, it will remind us that we are worth our own tears.

19

WE WAVE

*In which the author may be making too much
of a small, casual gesture by citing it as a symbol
of democracy—but he doesn't think so*

✳ ✳ ✳

This isn't one of the grander reasons for loving our country, but I'm not sure that it isn't as definite and grounded a reason as loving our country for its laws and guarantees. We wave. In the small Long Island village where I live and all over America, in fact, people wave to one another as a matter of course. I don't know if the gesture signals a kind of recognition. If so, it isn't personal, because we wave to total strangers. We take freedom for granted in America, because it is granted. And this affects our viscera in the most casual day-to-day interactions. I will be walking the dog. A hardware store truck or a fuel delivery truck turns the corner. The driver waves. I wave.

There is no way of proving the following contention, but I'd bet that everyone in my village has waved to everyone else at least once. Women wave more demonstratively—a lateral agitation of the forearm, not all that different from the taxi hail that says, in effect: "Stop everything. Here I am." Men keep it down, as a rule. A fellow dog-walker waves to me by slightly extending his arm to the right, then quickly draws it back. Another fellow gives a military salute. Another simply gives a herky-jerky nod of the head—his version of a wave. Me, I bend my arm and rotate my hand as if I were about to throw a curve.

Waving comes easily to me, if I say so myself. I have waved at people in Des Moines; Corpus Christie; Chicago; Great Falls, Montana; Montgomery, Alabama; Portland, Maine; Cleveland; St. Louis; Ann Arbor; Carefree, Arizona; all over. I've waved to cops, starlets, and athletes; to Yankee manager Joe Torre, Jamie Lee Curtis, and Alan Greenspan—none of whom I know. One of my earliest waves occurred when I was ten. I spotted the great old character actor Charles Coburn coming out of a building in my neighborhood, and I waved. He waved back. Had he not done that, who knows? I might have thought that waving to strangers was impolite, an imposition. But the gesture has always come naturally to me, to us, because in some way, it is less of a signal between citizens, than an expression of pleasure in simply being here and nowhere else.

So we identify ourselves to one another, principally because we don't have to (no checkpoints, you know; no papers). We simply go along in our fluent daily dance. Waves transmogrify to other small social events. At my local gas station, the owner and I talk baseball trades. At the local market, we talk hockey or the weather. When I do not know the person in a particular shop, there is usually some effort at communication. As I was paying for Chubby Hubby ice cream at the 7-Eleven the other night, the guy behind the counter reached over and flipped the on switch on a crazy-looking raccoon doll that sang "God Bless America." He laughed. I laughed.

Am I making too much of this? Possibly. People in rural places all over the world greet one another, and people in cities, including ours, generally do not. In the interests of accuracy, I must report that I have not always received wave for wave. But here, I think, we make contact—say hi, chat a bit, wave—as a celebration of nothing we have to think about, which, of course, is the beauty of it. And all it has taken to get this way is a monumental foundation, relentless vigilance, a brilliant code of laws, incomparable power, unshakable confidence in principles, and a historically unique civilization. Easy as pie.

20

WE'RE OLD-FASHIONED

*In which the author goes back to the America of his
childhood to visit three old ladies who cheated at canasta*

☆ ☆ ☆

Old-world America is where everyone lives first,
where we began our education, developed our prefer-
ences, literally came to our senses. It is no less part of the
country for existing only in memory. It is strange how
this works. One goes along in the ultra-present world of
Starbucks, teeth-whitening salons, computer cafés, and
so forth. But one lives simultaneously among the soda
fountains of one's youth and the double-decker buses
and the drive-ins. The country we belong to sits comfortably in both tenses.

My old world centered on three women, called spin-
sters in those days, who were in their seventies and early
eighties and who lived together in antique splendor in

the apartment directly above ours in the Gramercy Park neighborhood of New York. Miss Prescott was a librarian at Columbia University. Miss Jordan was a novelist and at one time had been an editor at *Harper's Bazaar* magazine. Miss Cutler was a painter and a potter. Her forebears came over on the *Mayflower*. It was she, I believe, who had the money.

They lived in a dark museum of an apartment with shields and swords on the walls and elephants carved out of ivory on the tables. At the age of five, I thought it noteworthy that people would carve ivory to make elephants, but I drew no conclusions. Framed coats of arms hung from wires on the ceilings. There was a freestanding suit of armor in the hall.

My mother, a junior-high-school English teacher, worked late in the afternoons, so I would go up the back stairs of the apartment house and visit the three ladies, who would be waiting for my arrival. They would read aloud to me—*The Wind in the Willows, Dr. Dolittle,* Jules Verne, Mark Twain. It was from Miss Prescott, Miss Jordan, and Miss Cutler that I learned the power of the written word. And also canasta; they taught me canasta (at which they openly cheated). Miss Jordan taught me how to play the piano. Well, not exactly *how* to play the piano, since she would attack the keys as if her hands were jackhammers. But she did teach me the notes for "Londonderry Air" and the "Blue Danube Waltz."

A five-year-old is in a pretty good position to assess who is beautiful and who is not. Removed from the confusions of sexuality, he or she can judge a face as a face. Miss Cutler's face was like her work: soft like pastels and soft like clay; a Helen Hayes–ish face. Miss Prescott's face was also like her work: square edged and bony. Her voice both sang and cracked. The face of Miss Jordan was huge and severe, a giant's face. Had her body been less than huge itself, it could not have supported her head. Her eyes were dark and keen, and she was always moving in a definite direction: toward the playing cards, toward the Steinway (boom!), toward a book.

Books made up the center of our afternoons—a reading, preceded by tea, and milk and cookies for me, the four of us seated around the coffee table, they chatting and nodding, I mostly watching and listening. It never occurred to me that the ladies had arranged the late part of their day to accommodate the schedule of a five-year-old boy. I thought that this was what they would do ordinarily—sit on the couch and read children's stories aloud. They were themselves so absorbed in the stories, so visibly excited about Tom Sawyer's white-washed fence and Mr. Toad's hall.

The shadows would lengthen in the dark museum, crawling on the antimacassars and the gold frames of the paintings. And I would watch the three of them travel into the kingdom of words and beckon me to join them.

Many years later, when I was teaching words myself, I came across a poem by John Crowe Ransom called "Blue Girls." The poem begins by calling attention to beautiful young girls and ends by recalling a withered old woman—"Yet it is not long / since she was lovelier than any of you." Of course, I thought of Miss Jordan, Miss Cutler, and Miss Prescott, by then long dead. I did not remember them with "perfections tarnished" but as perfectly lovely old women.

God, they could bicker! Miss Jordan used a broadsword, and the other two, rapiers. Politely, deftly, they would pass a teacup and remind one another of errors of judgment one of them had made, or worse, errors of fact. Miss Prescott the librarian was especially good at that. They were as alive to infighting as they were to the world of events. I did not always understand the substance of their quarrels, but I could tell that this was a more intriguing and stylish game than canasta, and I could see how they, who lived among swords and shields, embraced battle with both arms.

They lived for everything. For custom, for manners, for flowers, for newspapers, for literature, for warfare, for me.

On Christmas Eve, every Christmas Eve, they would hire a car to drive them up and down Fifth Avenue so that they could look at the displays in the shop windows. They took me with them. Slowly along the avenue the sleek black car would make its tour, the ladies sitting in the back, I in the front with the driver. They would point at the blazing windows and exclaim, rarely to me, and not exactly to one another. Each, on her own, was absorbed in something she had seen year after year, which was suddenly brand-new in her eyes. Sunk deep in the leather seat and staring straight ahead, I listened to them glow in the dark.

21

WE DIG THAT HOKEY, CORNY
PRESIDENTIAL TALK

In which the author makes an impassioned
yet dignified plea for more and more bullshit

☆ ☆ ☆

When Jackie Robinson was near death and blind from diabetes, he was given a day of celebration at Dodger Stadium. As Jackie was led back to the clubhouse, Jim Murray, the great sportswriter for the *Los Angeles Times,* touched him on the shoulder and identified himself. "Oh, Jim!" said Jackie. "I wish that I could see you again." Murray responded, "Jackie, I wish that I could see *you* again." Tom Callahan, another great sportswriter, told me that story.

Jackie Robinson comes to mind because not only did he embody the best of America while he fought off the worst but also because he always expressed a straightforward, unapologetic, sublimely corny love of country that is no longer heard in political rhetoric. "I believe in the human race," Robinson said. "I believe in the warm heart. I believe in the goodness of a free society. And I believe that the society can remain good only as long as we are willing to fight for it and to fight against whatever imperfections may exist."

Nobody in public life, certainly no candidate, talks that way anymore because this is a time of self-protective thinking. Candidates play defensive baseball to avoid errors, which is the surest way to make them. It is regarded as unsophisticated to discuss the fundamental nature of the country—either demonstrated or wished for—and so stump speeches consist of exquisitely balanced references to particular problems. Centrist politics leads to guarded expression. It also leads to an excessive emphasis on issues. The word "focused" is used as a compliment these days but where it means discipline, it just as often suggests tunnel vision. Political chatter to the contrary, I do not think that most people want to listen to speeches devoted to issues at all—or if they do, they quickly grow accustomed to (and bored by) the predictable positions a candidate takes. The "issue" that people never tire of is that of basic national principles and ambitions, the promotion of which, though usually couched in clichés, is eternally engaging because it touches us where we deeply live.

By far the stupidest reason for defensive political baseball is that the candidates are consciously talking to newspaper columnists and TV journalists, who are on the lookout only for flaws, in efforts to be clever, thus noticed. There's no trick in being clever and noticed; any deft young journalist can do it. Talking like Jackie Robinson, or like Ronald Reagan, our last sublimely corny president, takes more self-confidence and aggressive innocence but—providing that one means what one says—it pays off.

Our most cliché-ridden presidents were also our greatest ones. "Democracy," said Woodrow Wilson, "is more than a form of government. It is a form of character." Lincoln: "I hold that while man exists it is his duty to improve not only his own condition but to assist in ameliorating mankind." Lincoln was a supremely corny speaker—at least he would be judged so today. He began a noted speech at a battlefield with references to liberty and the proposition of equality. How hokey can you get?

As for FDR's speeches, they don't come much cornier

than his address on the four freedoms: "The first is freedom of speech and expression—everywhere in the world," he said. "The second is freedom of every person to worship God in his own way—everywhere in the world. The third is freedom from want, which, translated into world terms, means economic understandings which will secure to every nation a healthy peacetime life for its inhabitants—everywhere in the world. The fourth is freedom from fear, which, translated into world terms, means a worldwide reduction of armaments to such a point and in such a thorough fashion that no nation will be in a position to commit an act of physical aggression against any neighbor—anywhere in the world."

What former presidents seemed to understand was that often-repeated, hackneyed sentiments—if spoken by someone who really felt them—were, above everything, what Americans wanted to hear. Of course, we want to be told that something is going to be done about taxes (higher or lower), gun control (more or less), that the military will always be the strongest in the world, but not at the expense of "my highest priority" education or "my highest priority" health care or interest rates . . . *blah, blah, blah.* The odd thing is that such talk sounds more like *blah, blah, blah* than talk of relief for the poor, or of helping other nations in distress or of living up to our promise of *blah blah blah* equality.

The country was, always will be, a romance; to inspire, one has to presume a level of intimacy with its highest purposes. No audience believes what a candidate promises, and most significant events are cyclical, no matter who sits in the White House. Speak of fair play, unity, human rights, decency. You'll get us every time.

22

WE'RE NOBODY'S ALL-AMERICAN

*In which Ronald Reagan is recalled as an example
of both an ideal and the undesirability of achieving it*

* * *

The all-American boy is a strange character to hold up
as a reason for loving the country because, on the surface
of it, he is the sort of idealized figure that gets a country
into hot water. Other countries we can think of have
brought much grief to themselves and others by exalting
such a figure. But the nice thing about us is that while
promoting an American ideal with such fictional cre-
ations as Jack Armstrong in the 1940s, we never really
believed in him because he could not fit in with a civilization made up of differences. He was harmless, and he
was likable. And he was oddly useful because by his very
nonexistence he showed the only truly multicultural

country in world history that an ideal person was both impossible and undesirable.

The all-American boy said a good deal about our country's values, but he never said quite enough. He (it was always he, his counterpart being Miss America, who has undergone some makeovers herself) was courageous, honest, athletic, clean-cut, and modest. He could be charming as well and in a limited, self-deprecating way, even witty. But his all-Americaness was also stultifying. He could err but not sin, he could not display the normal range of low human reactions, he could not exhibit too much feeling. And he was dull. But the worst thing about him was that he imprisoned himself in a character that was, in fact, anti-American in its adamant and uniform perfection.

Ronald Reagan came close to being the all-American boy, and he suggested exactly why this ideal figure has gone the way of the flivver. I met him when I was writing *Time*'s "Man of the Year" story in 1980, the year of his election. It was a month before his inauguration, and he was at his home in Pacific Palisades, in Los Angeles. On the afternoon of my interview, he looked like a dream. He was wearing a blue-and-green wool tartan jacket, a purple tie, white shirt, white handkerchief, black pants, and black loafers with gold along the tops. Who else could dress that way? He settled back on a couch in a living room so splurged with color that even the black seemed exuberant. A florist must have decorated it. He was talking about job hunting as a kid in his hometown of Dixon, Illinois, telling an American success story he had told a hundred times before. He seemed genuinely happy to hear it again.

That was part of being the all-American boy; he told stories over and over—engagingly, expertly, yet never with too much force. At six-foot-one, he was hardly a small man, but he could will himself small so as not to be overwhelming or intrusive. Lyndon Johnson used to enter a room and rape it. Reagan seemed to be in a continual state of receding, a posture that made strangers lean toward him. In a contest for the same audience, he would have drawn better than Johnson.

The voice went perfectly with the body. No president since Kennedy had a voice at once so distinctive and beguiling. It, too, receded at the right moments, turning mellow at points of intensity. When it wished to be most persuasive, it hovered barely above a whisper so as to win you over by intimacy, if not by substance. This was style, but not sham. Reagan believed everything he said no matter how often he said it, even if he used the same words every time. He liked his voice, treated it like a guest. He made you part of his hospitality.

He told me about one of his football games at Eureka College—one that he later rebroadcast on the radio: "So when the light went on I said, 'Here we are going into the fourth quarter on a cold November afternoon, the long, blue shadows settling over the field, the wind whipping in through the end of the stadium'—hell, we didn't have a stadium at Eureka, we had grandstands—and I took it up to the point in which there were twenty seconds to go and we scored the winning touchdown. As a blocking guard, I was supposed to get the first man in the secondary to spring our back loose, and I didn't get him. I missed him. And I've never known to this day how Bud Cole got by and scored that touchdown. But in the rebroadcast I nailed the guy on defense. I took him down with a magnificent block."

Cheers and laughter. Who would not hire such a man? In many ways, his presidency was like the football story. He made it up as he went along. During his years in the White House, he used to tell anecdotes derived from movie scenes that he seemed to believe had really happened. He told a tale of America that he deeply believed to be true as well. In terms of raising the national mood, the tale came true. He told the Soviet Union to tear down the Berlin Wall, so it did. He told it to collapse and go away, and it did that, too. In short, his fictive vision of the world was so sincere and unswerving that he brought the world around to seeing it. And all the while, he remained courageous, honest, athletic, clean-cut, and modest.

Hidden within his all-Americanism, however, was the life that made him human—his divorce from Jane Wyman, his alcoholic father, his own strange distance from everyone except Nancy. When I was preparing to interview him, I discovered that his son Mike said that Reagan had never gone to any of his football games. I also read that Reagan, too, had mentioned that his own father was guilty of the same neglect. Reagan hadn't attended any of his other son Ron's ballet performances, either. And he kept his daughters at arm's length as well. So I asked him about all this, and suddenly his face went pale. Mainly he looked confused. He had been caught in a human imperfection. He did not have a ready-made story for this contingency, and he did not know his lines.

It is a crushing burden to be all-American, which is why few people would want to assume the mantle, even if that were possible. One does not need to go as far with it as the Nazis did for an idealized figure to cause a great deal of damage. The mere promotion of such a figure— a falsity in itself—promotes falsity in others and no small degree of pain. Who's nose is the perfect nose? Who is my perfect little boy? In a way, the ideal form is analogous to school prayer. There is nothing really wrong with it, but it leaves certain people out and we're not supposed to do that.

Reagan grew up with Jack Armstrong and similar fictions, and it was natural for him to aspire to be like them. Jay Gatsby did the same thing. But I always felt that Reagan assumed his role only halfheartedly; the children of alcoholics grow up knowing explosive anger and sudden fear. To be as good as gold is a way to ward off anarchy. Whatever one thought of his politics, Reagan was a heroic man. He would have been as heroic or more without the encumbrance of an ideal. In moments of self-inspection, he probably would have been happier as well.

And we are happier without it, too. Which is why— slowly and without comment—we got rid of the all-

American boy as an ideal image. No single uniform image replaced it, either. That was the point. The only all-Americans you hear about these days are athletes, and even they are in short supply because everyone goes pro as soon as possible. Ideal figures are trouble. In their place are the rest of us—all of us, really—stumbling about and making a perfect mess of things.

23

BASICALLY, WE'RE OUT
OF THIS WORLD

In which we digress

✷ ✷ ✷

The teachers would catch me dreaming out the window and ask the shrill, predictable question: "Roger, would you care to rejoin the class?" I would think, "Not really" as I swiveled reluctantly toward planet Earth. Unconsciously, I was operating within a major American tradition. People on other continents assume that because we are a can-do nation, we are also a want-to-do one, but we aren't. For all our reputation for being with it, Americans—in our free and sauntering souls—are just as often in outer space. Not for nothing was the American Dream created, and along with it, a population of idlers who would much prefer to be out of things than in them.

And why not? One of the odder charms of our country is that most of us—the great majority—not only feel out of things; we hardly know anyone who thinks of him or herself as *in* things. If presidential candidates are to be believed, not one of them has ever set foot in Washington, D.C. Candidates who are former congressmen or senators must have driven around the periphery of the city on the Beltway, tossing in their votes from their cars. Washington is known as the city of insiders. To be an insider—the term implies—is not just to be where the power is, but to be wrong in one's perspective, perhaps even to be a crook. Thus being an outsider is a form of self-congratulation. Only the best people do it.

One of the splendid tensions within which we function is the one between overworking and overdreaming. Part of the reason I myself work like crazy is to make amends for a personality that would have gladly spent its life staring out the window. This tendency has its penalties, as you might imagine. In the sixth grade, our teacher, having momentarily forced me to rejoin the class, asked anyone who had a musical instrument to bring it in and play it. As it happened, my aunt had bought me a guitar the day before, and though I had never played the guitar,

I thought I'd do a few numbers. The next day I sat before my classmates, whose rising laughter nearly drowned out my one-chord rendition of "Red River Valley." I just assumed that if I sat up there with my guitar, the ability to play it would come to me.

Some distinguished figures justify this removed way of life. In "Memories of West Street and Lepke," Robert Lowell lamented, "I was so out of things," to indicate he was praising the condition. Unhappily, one of the things he was out of was his mind. In the movie *Humoresque,* Oscar Levant told Joan Crawford, "Don't blame me, lady. I didn't make the world. I barely live on it." Somerset Maugham dignified the dreaming-out-the-window business. "A state of reverie," he said, "does not avoid reality; it accedes to reality."

Maugham's notion suggests that being out of things is a way of seeing the things one is out of more clearly. Like the old visual puzzle that showed nine dots in the shape of a square, and you had to connect them all in a single diagram without lifting your pen from the paper. The solution was to draw the connecting lines starting outside the dots.

Like Holden Caulfield in speech class, when the kids were taught to yell out "Digression!" at anyone who got off point, the point of which is . . . But the whole point of being out of things is not to justify it, not to profess any grand intentions. Holden never felt the need to explain himself. Neither did Huck Finn or Tom Sawyer, or the boy in Winslow Homer's painting with the weed in his teeth, or any of the great American dreamers.

Would you care to rejoin the class? Would you care to rejoin the program in progress? Would you care to re-join Cokie and Sam and Tim and Wolf? (I wish that Wolf were on Fox.) Would you care to rejoin the parties, the pollsters, the civil service, the Civil War, the Elks, Moose, Masons, Mummers, the American Legion, the French Foreign Legion, the Boy Scouts, the team, the league, the gang, the clique, band, guild, the company, the task force, the committee, the subcommittee, the staff, the tribe, sect, clan, caste, phylum, genus, species? The presidential race? The human race? Not really.

That's part of the reason that being out of things feels so good to us—because we are not joiners by na-ture, temperament, or history. James Fenimore Cooper's novel *Satanstoe* envisaged an entire nation made up of grand, lush, private estates, separated from one another by miles. (Nice estate if you can get it.) But even in our more realistic America, people want to keep to their own thoughts, wishes, flights. The nation was founded by outsiders and with an outsider mentality. Only a true outsider can be a cowboy, an inventor, a hero. The country itself was made up out of a dream—producing, some would say, a dream of a country. I'm sorry. What were you saying?

Outside the window, the day breaks over a red Schwinn bike that powers itself toward the smiling sun. The ball game is about to begin. Someone is handing out free guitars and chocolate shakes. School's out. And I am watching Ashley Judd walk very slowly, but definitely, toward me.

24

ANNIE DROPS HER GUN
(SMILE WHEN YOU SAY THAT)

*In which the author, heaving with sunny optimism
as usual, declares that one more reason for loving the country
is that it's about to dump its weapons. Wanna bet on it?*

✳ ✳ ✳

The way we sometimes wind up doing the right thing
in this country is to squat in the wrong place for a hundred years or so, then spring to our feet suddenly, ready
to move forward. That's what happened with civil rights,
and it's what's going to happen with gun control. Count
on it. As terrible as Columbine was, as terrible as all the
school, office, and street killings of the past few years
have been, I'm pretty sure that the country is going
through the literal death throes of a barbaric era and that
mercifully soon, one of these monstrous episodes will be

the last. My guess, in fact, is that the hour has come and gone—that the great majority of Americans are saying they favor gun control when they really mean gun banishment. Trigger locks, waiting periods, purchase limitations, which may seem important corrections at the moment, will soon be seen as mere tinkering with a machine that is as good as obsolete. Marshall McLuhan said that by the time one notices a cultural phenomenon, it has already happened. We'll keep the hunting rifles and shotguns. But I think that we are more than ready to get rid of the rest of the damn things—the handguns, the semis, and the automatics.

Those who claim otherwise tend to cite America's enduring love affair with guns, but there never was one. The image of shoot-'em-up America was mainly the invention of the gunmaker Samuel Colt, who managed to convince a malleable nineteenth-century public that no household was complete without a firearm—"an armed society is a peaceful society." This ludicrous aphorism turned two hundred years of Western tradition on its ear. Until 1850, fewer than ten percent of U.S. citizens had guns. Only fifteen percent of violent deaths between 1800 and 1845 were caused by guns. Reputedly wide-open western towns, such as Dodge City and Tombstone, had strict gun-control laws; guns were confiscated at the Dodge City limits.

If the myth of a gun-loving America is merely the product of gun salesmen, dime novels, movies, and the NRA—which, incidentally, was not opposed to gun control until the 1960s, when gun buying sharply increased—it would seem that creating a gun-free society would be fairly easy. But Americans themselves, in one of our episodes of national idiocy, have retarded such progress by positing an absurd connection between guns, personal power, freedom, and beauty. The old Western novels established a shoot-'em-up corollary to the Declaration of Independence by depicting the cowboy as a moral loner who preserves the peace and his own honor by shooting faster and surer than the competition. The old gangster movies gave us opposite versions of the same character. Scarface is simply an illegal Lone Ranger, with the added element of success in the free market. Stupid, but appealing.

To be fair, it should be acknowledged that gun control is one of those issues that is simultaneously simpler and more complicated than it appears. Advocates usually point to Britain, Australia, and Japan as their models, where guns are restricted and crime is reduced. They do not point to Switzerland, where there is a gun in every home and crime is practically nonexistent. Then there are the constitutional questions. In a way, the anti-gun movement mirrors the humanitarian movement in international politics. Bosnia, Kosovo, Rwanda, and, in a way, Afghanistan have suggested that the West, the U.S. in particular, is heading toward a politics of human rights that supersedes the politics of established frontiers and, in some cases, laws. Substitute private property for frontiers and the Second Amendment for laws, and one begins to see that the politics of humanitarianism requires a trade-off involving the essential underpinnings of American life. To tell Americans what they can or cannot own or do in their homes is always a tricky business. As for the Second Amendment, it may pose an inconvenience for gun-control advocates, but no more an inconvenience than the First Amendment offers those who blame violence on movies and television.

Gun-control forces also ought not to make reform an implicit attack on people who like and own guns. Urban liberals ought to be especially alert to the cultural bigotry that categorizes such people as hicks, racists, psychotics, and so forth. For one thing, a false moral superiority is impractical and incites a backlash among people otherwise sympathetic to sensible gun control, much like the backlash the abortion rights forces incurred once their years of political suasion had ebbed. And the demonizing of gun owners or even the NRA is simply wrong. The majority of gun owners are as dutiful, responsible, and sophisticated as most of their taunters.

That said, I am pleased to report that the likelihood of sweeping and lasting changes in the matter of America and guns has never been higher. There comes a time in every civilization when people have had enough of a bad thing, and the difference between this moment and previous spasms of reform is that it springs from the grassroots and is not driven by politicians, legal institutions, or charismatic leaders. Gun-control sentiment is everywhere in the country these days—except in the Bush White House. It surfaces in the courts and in the gun industry itself, which, having lost suits in several cities, has seen the light and begun to police itself. But it seems nowhere more conspicuous than in the villages, the houses of worship, and the consensus of the kitchen. More grassroots groups against guns emerged in 1999 than ever before, and they keep coming.

One must remember, however, that the NRA, too, is a grassroots organization. Its true effectiveness exists in small local communities where one or two thousand votes can swing an election. People who own guns and who ordinarily might never vote at all become convinced that their freedoms, their very being, will be jeopardized if they do not vote Smith in and Jones out. They are the defense-oriented "little guys" of the American people, beset by Big Government, big laws, and rich liberals who want to take away the only power they have.

They are convinced, of course, of something wholly untrue—that the possession of weapons gives them stature, makes them more American. This idea, too, was a Colt-manufactured myth, indeed, an ad slogan: "God may have made men, but Samuel Colt made them equal." Still crazy, after all these years. If equality depended on guns instead of laws, Martin Luther King would have wanted to be armed to the teeth.

Lasting social change usually occurs when people decide to do something they know they ought to have done long ago but have kept the knowledge private. This, I believe, is what happened with civil rights, and it is happening with guns. I doubt that it will be twenty-five years before we're rid of the things. In ten years, even five, we could be looking back on the past three decades of gun violence in America the way one once looked back upon eighteenth-century madhouses. I mean, exactly the same way.

25

WE'RE NOT THAT INNOCENT

*In which a line from a Britney Spears song is
adopted to indicate how hip the author is and to
make a point about national virtue*

✶ ✶ ✶

People said that we were shocked by the attacks of September 11 because we're an innocent country. But except in the narrowest definition of innocence—being taken by surprise by an aerial attack—there has never been anything innocent about us. What's more, we know it. We consistently, and justifiably, beat ourselves up over a history of Indian slaughter, slavery, the crushing of workers, the abandonment of the poor, child labor, blacklists, poll taxes, segregation, the harassment of homosexuals, anti-everyone behavior, the internment camps, the suppression of women, My Lai. Shall I go on? A nation with a history that includes such events only regards itself as innocent as a bit of convenient folklore. But we use the word, nonetheless, to reestablish the vision of the ideal state, like the untrammeled virginal American landscape, that allows us to think of ourselves as a better people than some of our history might indicate.

This, in fact, is a very good idea. Out of a yearning for a moral Eden, the forward motion of other, brighter history is born. Recall *Brown* v. *Board of Education.* In the early 1950s, Linda Brown, an African-American fifth grader in Topeka, Kansas, was denied admission to a white elementary school. The NAACP took up her case and similar cases in South Carolina, Delaware, and Virginia. The case was argued by Thurgood Marshall in 1952 and was finally ruled on by the Supreme Court on May 17, 1954. The ruling, simply and clearly, was that the "separate but equal" clause in *Plessy* v. *Ferguson* (1896) violated the children's Fourteenth Amendment rights. And with that decision, bad law was made good.

It seemed to me so easily done at the time. I was thirteen, and I remember thinking (when I did any thinking at all at that age): "What's the big deal?" The big deal was that *Brown* did not simply right a wrong law; it exposed, and thus held up to contempt, a widespread assumption that blacks were inferior people. The assumption had been a guilty, not-so-secret American secret. It did not arise out of innocence, but neither could it have been obliterated by innocence. Only because the country had been challenged and made aware of its sinfulness or moral laziness was it able, at last, to do the right thing.

There is a different route that nations can take when they want to make up for guilty episodes. They can make public apologies. France did that when it owned up to its collaboration with the Nazis against its Jewish citizens. The Vatican, too, though cagily, has "acknowledged" its history of anti-Semitism. Japan has apologized (sort of) for its abominable treatment of Koreans and Chinese. And we ourselves have apologized for the Japanese-American internment camps, for slavery, for our treatment of the Indians.

All of which is very nice and commendable, but also a little silly and wholly without effect. What do you say, dear, after you've said you're sorry? This recent spate of international apologies makes me wonder how the Vandals would have apologized to the Romans. (We're very sorry for our vandalism?) How would Alexander and Tamburlaine have expressed contrition? The most effective apology for something in the past is to correct something in the present. Thus *Brown*. Thus Title Nine. Thus the laws concerning the handicapped. Thus *Miranda*.

None of these corrections could have come to pass in an innocent nation (whatever that might be), but they would not have had to, either. What powerful nation—what nation, for that matter—could possibly be innocent? One reason to love our country, in fact, is that we do not take innocence as seriously as we claim to, which allows us to attempt to make use of experience. We may express *Casablanca* shock when we're caught in a wrong, but sooner or later, we try to fix what's broken. Sometimes it is very much later. Between *Plessy v. Ferguson* and *Brown* came fifty-eight years.

I do not mean to dwell on *Brown* as an example of our being reborn on the spot and instantly cleansed, but rather the opposite. After *Brown*, the country did not join hands and sing "Black and White Together." There was Selma, there was Birmingham. There were church bombings and civil rights workers murdered and children clubbed in the streets. Forty years after *Brown*, in 1994, a Harvard study named New York State among the most segregated in the country, and the most segregated for Latino students. The laws were in place, but neighborhoods were segregated, and they still are. The country has a very long way to go in race relations. And the means to that end involve continuous strife—progress, setbacks, crime, self-recrimination, progress. But it helps to live in a free country. Theologian Reinhold Niebuhr had it nailed: "Our capacity for justice makes democracy possible, and our capacity for injustice makes democracy necessary."

But the impulse to clean up our act at all could never derive from a state of innocence. America has been through the mill—often one of our own manufacture. Innocence is a preposterous and useless condition: first, because it makes a people vulnerable; second, because no improvement can come of it. The test of a civilization is not that it struggles against poverty and need. The test of a civilization is that it struggles against itself—its guilty, sinful, human self. The balance of powers created by the Constitution was a clear statement of low expectations. We have frequently lived up to them.

2 6

WE'RE MIGHTY PURTY

In which the sheer beauty of the country is noted,
suggesting that the best argument for preserving
the environment is the environment

☆ ☆ ☆

Country like this could bring out anything in a
man—ecstasy, murder, grace. I grow aware of this as I
follow Yvon Chouinard along the rocks down an off-
shoot of the Snake River, in Wyoming's Jackson Hole, in
the Grand Tetons. Chouinard, sixty, the president and
founder of Patagonia, the outdoor clothing and gear
company based in Ventura, California, that seems more
interested in protecting the environment than its prof-
its, is about to teach me fly-fishing. Ahead of us, the
quicksilver water burbles and shushes. Across the river,
the cold mountains, patched with snowfields and dark
bruises, poke into a hot, dry sky more white than blue.

This is the real and only appeal of fishing to me. I realize that to be "gone fishin'" is an important American custom—the aggressive declaration of vacation in the land of the stressful. But I've taken less pleasure in the sport—which, until my trip with Chouinard, was confined to the deep-sea variety (which he dismisses contemptuously with the phrase "with worms!")—than I have in simply being near water. My time with him has the same reward: a few hours in the company of the beauty of the country.

All this is new to me. Even the Rockies look different here, more brooding and stuck up. At the local store, where we got our one-day licenses, I noted the names of the flies for sale: Ausable Wulff, Hare's Ear, Cook's Rug, Wild Muddler. Wild Muddler appealed to me. Chouinard—small and tightly built, with the forearms of the blacksmith he once was—wears green canvas sneakers with holes, a pair of yellowed sweat socks, denim shorts, a beat-up cap, a Patagonia vest, of course, and a T-shirt bearing the words "cutthroat businessman." It is a reference to the cutthroat trout he'd like to catch (named for the red slash across its throat) and to the antithesis of the sort of businessman he is. He glides from rock to rock like the champion mountain climber he also once was, while I muddle wildly, tottering like a top at the end of its spin, tangling my fishing line and attempting to heed my instructor.

"It's all about process," he says, "fly-fishing and everything else." To fish with a fly is to imitate the fly at its various stages of development. As the fly is born and grows, it changes at different times of the day and year. Sometimes the fish go for the nymph, the youngest stage, at the bottom of the river. Sometimes they wait for the flies when they are emerging upward, attached to a self-created gas bubble. When the fly matures, it lies helpless on the top of the water until the bubble explodes and frees its wings. The fish will try for it then, too, and you imitate that stage with a dry fly on the surface. It's a matter of educating yourself—about the insects, fish, and water. "It's all about process."

He begins my education by showing me dry-fly casting on a path above the river. Move the arm, not the wrist; keep the arc of the cast between two and ten o'clock. But today the fish we are going for, whitefish and cutthroats, are loitering on the bottom. So we will wet cast and roll cast instead, with little weights on the lines and flies that look like nymphs. Roll casting requires less arm movement. You swing the line upriver and let it drift down in a natural motion. I find I'm not half bad at this, thanks wholly to Chouinard, who is as aware of the process in teaching as in everything else.

After twenty minutes of correcting and watching me, he suddenly leaves, and I do not notice him leaving. Now I am alone, standing on a flat gray rock in the Snake River, roll casting, as if I had walked there by myself. Out goes the line, like a river winding on a river. The fly whips and curls. I strip the line. I am beginning to see what he means by process. It is far more satisfying to cast for a fish than to have one on your hook. The consequence completes the process, so it is necessary to the process. But it also carries a kind of disappointment in completion.

Ah. I catch four whitefish, one after the other, and throw them back.

"Four's a good number," he tells me. "We'll say you caught a few. It'll sound like more." We watch an air show. An osprey scares off a bald eagle that has probably come too close to its nest.

I don't know much about nature, but I know what I like about the American landscape. I know what everybody knows about what we're doing wrong about the environment—sixty percent of the rain forests lost to agriculture or timber interests, global warming gases, PCBs in rivers. All urgent and important matters. But to me, the best argument for protecting the country is the way it looks as country. That, and the feel of overwhelming, intimidating, expanding liberation. The "issue" of the environment is taken up by the environment itself.

I ask Chouinard if the joy he takes in fishing relates to operations at Patagonia. He says that from the outset in the early 1970s, the entire goal of the company was to do the right thing. At first it meant making the most useful and durable products, the best. Chouinard's company produced aluminum chocks instead of the old steel pitons for climbing, so the rocks would not be scarred. It was also the first outdoors company to introduce modern synthetic fleece. These days he is leading a fight to dismantle some of the nation's hydroelectric dams, once essential for people, now harmful to spawning salmon.

He admits it's not easy for a business to be green. "But part of the process of life is to question how you live it. Nobody takes the time to do things right. Look at those guys." He indicates three boats that have appeared on the river. Two fishermen sit on raised chairs at the bow and stern of each boat. A guide sits in the middle and rows. "They won't catch a thing," says Chouinard, "because they're dry casting. Besides, you don't need a boat to fish this goddamn river. All summer I haven't seen one other person walking the river." Chouinard is dead on; the men don't catch a single fish among them.

Failing to focus sufficiently on process, I hand him my fishing line, which I now have tangled into the shape of a bird's nest, a condor's. He begins to work at it with saintly patience, then to my great relief, shows normal human frustration by letting out an expletive that has to do with maternity and copulation.

I tell him, "I was beginning to worry about you—too serene."

"Nah," he laughs, "I'm just another dirtbag. But a rich dirtbag."

At day's end, I watch him walk to the river and begin casting with so deft a motion it seems he is drawing currents in the air. After a few casts, he hooks a female cutthroat that shimmers gold and silver as it resists and bends his rod into a bow. When he pulls in the fish, it wriggles under the arc of the bow before he moves it toward his hand. The trout looks up at him in desperate wonder. He reaches for its mouth and sets it free.

27

I VERMONT, YOU VERMONT,
WE VERMONT

In which a very special state is singled out as the
embodiment of our nonsensical pursuit of unhappiness

* * *

Let us now praise famous states—one state, at least—
for a quality that reflects a national characteristic. I speak
of Vermont. Vermont is the thing one desperately wants
when one desperately does not want it. In this sense, it
is also representative of the cycles of American consumerism—the practice in which we touchingly seek
everything we do not need and then, when we get it, re-
gret it. Our pursuit of happiness makes us optimistic, but
our pursuit of unhappiness makes us lovable.

I've thought about Vermont a lot. When Sunday's
New York Times thuds on the doorstep, I immediately
nosedive into the "Farms & Country Homes" real estate

section, poking about for "colonial with barn on thirty acres, mostly in field." This is no idle pursuit with me. Ginny and I bought, lived in, and, after an interminable year, eagerly sold a 1785 colonial with barn on thirty acres, mostly in field. You'd think that once having tasted paradise and spat it out that one would not seduce oneself into the same delusionary dream for a second time. But Vermont is the thing one desperately wants when one desperately does not want it.

I repeat that observation only to emphasize Vermont's unique cooperation with an uncorrectable flaw in the American makeup: When it comes to romance, experience is no teacher. To the contrary, there are certain experiences that prove the more tantalizing the more disappointing they are. The Chicago Cubs, soufflé desserts, and Congress are cases in point.

What makes Vermont the most brilliant exemplar of this self-punishing romanticism is that under its sylvan disguise of colonial barns and fieldy acres, the state is an exceptionally weird place. In 1990, in a series of seven town meetings in seven different towns, the great majority of Vermonters voted to secede from the Union. For Vermonters such behavior is normal. Other facts of interest:

1. After the Green Mountain Boys of Bennington captured Fort Ticonderoga at the outset of the Revolutionary War, Vermont not only refused to help its fellow colonies in the struggle, but declared itself an independent republic in 1777. General Washington considered invading the place.

2. In the War of 1812, some Vermonters fought the British, while a good many more Vermonters smuggled cattle to them.

3. The Vermont legislature declared war against Germany in September 1941, three months before the rest of the country decided to follow suit.

4. Matthew Lyon of Vermont, a U.S. congressman, was reelected while serving time in jail for sedition.

5. Among Vermont's proud list of "firsts" is the news that Horace Wells of White River Junction was the first person to use laughing gas as an anesthetic for pulling teeth (1844). Since every business transaction in Vermont, such as buying a pack of Chiclets, may be compared to pulling teeth, Mr. Wells's "first" must have been much appreciated.

6. Most recently, Vermont senator Jim Jeffords switched parties from Republican to Democrat. This sort of behavior stunned the country, but no one in Vermont noticed.

Rather than dissuading outsiders from the utopian dream of Vermont living, the queer doings of Vermonters have mightily enhanced the state's attractiveness. Since Vermont is the thing one wants when one desperately does not want it, the desire to be part of a collection of rarefied oddballs has proved irresistible, especially to middle European immigrants and their kin and to dissident Russians like Alexander Solzhenitsyn, who like to think of heaven as solitary orneriness, mostly in field. Only when one has actually taken the plunge does it occur that there may be more to life than sledding in a Currier & Ives print. It is then that one packs up and hurries out of the state toward New York, where the *Times* awaits, advertising "Farms & Country Homes."

You might say that Vermont is the emblem not only of American consumerism but also of a permanent human yearning that is best served when it remains unsatisfied. To *vermont*—it ought to be a verb (transitive)—is to not want by wanting. The verb should be used only in extremely cautionary circumstances. Samson vermonted after Delilah. After Lyndon Johnson, anti-Vietnam war activists vermonted after Nixon.

Where does one do one's vermonting? In the yearning for cosmetic surgery, when you wind up with a face that looks as natural as a landscape for a model railroad? In the longing to own a Porsche 928S and rev up to a speed-limited 55 mph on the freeway, while your car depreciates to half its original cost? In the ambition to play shortstop for the Dodgers and at age thirty-five, to have your very own used-car dealership for the last fifty years of your life, where, incidentally, you will retag your old Porsche every week?

At the ripe young age of eighteen, I was sitting in a bar (legal in those days), nursing a beer I didn't like the taste of and killing time by daydreaming, when entered a Hollywoody redhead who made my heart gulp. Grown up at last, with a draft card as evidence, I thought: *If only I could lure that lollapalooza to my side, what a wild sweaty night we would have.* I tossed her my most manly look (she was twenty-five if a day), which she greeted with the enthusiasm of someone receiving notice of an income-tax penalty. But then, to my astonishment, she walked over to where I was internally panting.

"Wanna gosum place?" the beauty throatily asked.

"Me?" I stammered in soprano.

"Wanna gitoutaheah?" asked the vision.

"Gosh," I said. "I'd love to. But I, uh … I have, uh … an appointment." I overpaid for my beer and left the bar as fast as one could walk without sprinting.

Breathing easier outside, I looked back through the picture window and watched the redhead take the seat where I'd been sitting and finish my beer in a swig. Never in my life had I seen anything so shapely, so perfect of feature, so available, and unavailable. How I vermonted to reenter the bar.

Many years passed before I laid eyes on that woman again. It was in the Sunday *New York Times* real estate section. She had changed her appearance dramatically. I know that it's hard to believe, but she had turned into a colonial with barn on thirty acres, mostly in field.

2 8

WE PLAY BALL

*In which the author produces the mandatory essay
praising baseball in order to try to make a larger point
about America's need to stay young. Does he do it?*

✳ ✳ ✳

It is the second summer of the baseball season that re-
veals the game's complete nature. The second summer
does not have the blithe optimism of the first half of the
season. From August to the Series a sense of mortality
begins to lower over the game—a suspicion that will
deepen by late September to a certain knowledge that
something that was bright, lusty, and overflowing with
possibility can come to an end.

The beauty of the game is that it traces the arc of
American life. Until mid-August, baseball was a boy in
shorts whooping it up on the fat grass. Now it becomes

a leery veteran with a sun-baked neck, whose main concern is to protect the plate. In its second summer, baseball is about fouling off death. Sadaharu Oh, the Babe Ruth of Japanese baseball, wrote an ode to his sport in which he praised the warmth of the sun and foresaw the approaching change to "the light of winter coming."

But the whole point of baseball is to hold off the light of winter coming, at least to give keeping it at bay a shot. Several years ago, the Yankees' Darryl Strawberry, slumping and in need of personal redemption, hit three home runs in a row in a game with the White Sox and was temporarily redeemed. First and last, baseball is about the individual. In other sports it is the ball that does the scoring. In baseball the person scores. The game was designed to center on Americans in our individual strivings.

The runner on first has a notion to steal second. The first baseman has a notion to slip behind him. The pitcher has a notion to pick him off, but he delivers to the plate where the batter swings to protect the runner who decides to go now, and the second baseman braces himself to make the tag if only the catcher can rise to the occasion and put a low, hard peg on the inside third of the bag.

Fans cling to the glory moments of the game's history because such memories preserve everybody's summer light. Hey. Will you ever forget Yogi Berra fastened to Don Larsen's chest after Larsen's perfect game? Hey. Bobby Thompson's three-run homer against the Dodgers, Ted Williams's homer in his last at bat. Say hey. Willie Mays's catch of Vic Wertz's drive to center at the Polo Grounds.

Bring out the photo album of recollected parts: Bob Gibson's scowl, Stan Musial's shy smile, Junior Gilliam's wrists, Mickey Mantle's back, Don Mattingly's sloping shoulders. Play back the voice of Mel Allen, the Yankee announcer who died a few years ago, his very name a waterfall of *l*'s rolling out over the radio on an eternal afternoon. "Hello, everybody. This is Mel Allen."

All meld into emotions that attempt to live forever. It was not only that Willie turned his back and took off. It was the green continent of grass on which he ran and the waiting to see if he would catch up with the ball and the reek of your sweat and of everyone else's who sat like Seurat dots in the stadium, in the carved-out bowl of a planet that shines pale in daylight, bright purple and emerald at night.

It always comes down to the fundamental confrontation of pitcher and batter, with the catcher involved as the only player who faces the field and sees the whole game; he presides as a masked god squatting. The pitcher's role is slyer than the batter's, but the batter's is more human. The pitcher plays offense and defense simultaneously. He labors to tempt and to deceive. The batter cannot know what is coming. He can go down swinging or looking and be made to appear the fool. Yet he has a bat in his hands. And if all goes well and he can accomplish that most difficult feat in sports by hitting a small, hard sphere traveling at 90 mph with a heavy rounded stick, well then, fate is thwarted for a moment and the power over life is his. The question ought not to be, Why do the greatest hitters connect successfully only a third of the time? It ought to be, How do they get a hit at all?

So it goes for as many seasons as one is allowed; then the ability to play wanes. But things often get best just before the end. They say that forty-one-year-old Ozzie Smith, the great Cardinals shortstop, should have quit before he had to suffer the emergence of a better, younger fielder. Watching the All-Star game in 1996, one might have agreed when Ozzie let a high chopper play him that he would have charged without blinking a few years earlier. But then he made a classic double-play pivot in the sixth and beamed like a kid.

29

LET US NOW PRAISE FAMOUS CITIES

*In which it is pointed out that the Bronx is up
and the Battery down—but not out*

✳ ✳ ✳

A homeless man known to me as Charlie, who was only a little crazier than the rest of us, decided to set up a living room a few years ago on the sidewalk outside the church at Eighty-sixth and Amsterdam. He had scavenged a spotted sofa, two end tables, a BarcaLounger stuck in the recline position, a rug that had probably been orange in the 1960s, and a standing lamp that plugged into nothing. It was a pretty nice-looking place, and since I knew Charlie from the neighborhood, I sat down in his outdoor room to talk. After a while, it was clear that I was boring him. "Well, Roger," he said through his four remaining teeth. "I've enjoyed this chat. But I'm expecting guests."

The skinny on New York City is that you'd want to visit, but never live there. A friend of mine, and fellow New Yorker, told me that she thinks just the opposite is true. So do I. I'd go as far as to claim (as Dr. Johnson did for London) that until you have lived in New York, you haven't lived. The city is a reason to love America in part because it is a distillation of American ambitions. It also shows what happens when those ambitions are distributed among eight million people living in tight and steely quarters.

After September 11, the city, seeking to revive the trust of tourists, began a series of TV ads. Elegant pitchmen from the mayor on down sold the city to tourists as a warm and welcoming town, soaring with resilience and with dreams. New York is some of those things, sometimes, but that is not why millions come to stay. The reason people love the city is that it is difficult to live here. Come visit New York and observe a strange grace born of a hard and crazy life.

On my way to work a few years ago, I used to pass a street beggar who made his appeals by displaying a dog and a cat. "That's not much of an attraction," I suggested to him. "I know," he said. "I used to have a duck, but the duck quit the act."

Welcoming? On the first day my grandparents arrived at St. Mark's Place via Ellis Island, they were welcomed by robbers who stole every little thing they had. Young people who come to the city today are welcomed just as lavishly, with unaffordable apartments and ungettable jobs. They come, nonetheless, because whether they know it or not, they are looking for trouble—trouble of the strengthening kind. When they deal with it successfully, they change into New Yorkers: people who tend to possess a comic and enduring calm.

So yes, the place is resilient, but that was demonstrated long before September 11. It takes a crazy courage to live here. H. G. Wells recognized this as early as 1907, when he wrote *The War in the Air*—in which, by the way, he predicted that New York would suffer aerial bombardment in the first war of the "scientific age." (This was also when airplanes were still only a rumor.) Wells wrote that New York was the most likely target because "she was too strong to be occupied and too undisciplined and proud to surrender in order to escape destruction."

People say that the city is a microcosm of the country, but in many ways it is friendlier (yep, that's what I said) than a lot of the country. Different peoples get along better in New York than they do most anywhere else because of a kind of shared civilized wildness born of compression. Deep within their overtaxed hearts, New Yorkers live comfortably with a thrilling irrationality. The city itself is hard to believe.

September 11 showed what the city is made of. But in less dramatic times, as well, the New York way of life mixes difficulty with patience (belied by a surface irritability) to produce a unique sort of stamina. The ads by celebrities claim the city for dreamers. But most New Yorkers are not consistently driven by dreams. The dream was to get here in the first place. Most people are more than content to just make it home every evening.

I loved growing up here. The city is for walkers, and as a kid I'd walk everywhere—to school; to the movies (thirty blocks uptown); to St. Mark's Place where, in the summers, my grandparents and their cronies would sit on folding chairs on the sidewalks and gossip in Yiddish; down to the Village, where my friends and I would play basketball and stoop ball (no one was better than Nunzio Pernaconio); back up to Central Park, the amazing rectangular oasis dreamed up by Frederick Law Olmstead, who in the mid-nineteenth century foresaw that one day boxed-in New Yorkers would long for a patch of grass. And there were the shadowed, empty streets of warehouses, and the scary silence. And the sudden tulips in the snow.

"How much can New Yorkers take?" was a question heard after a plane crashed in the Rockaways in mid-November after the World Trade Center attacks. The whole process of taking constitutes half of what the city is about. The other half consists of what it offers by example to the rest of the world, which is akin to what the country often offers as well. I always thought that George Washington moved the nation's capital from New York southward because he saw that the city would be too big merely for the center of America. New York is the capital of the world, not because of its wealth and influence, but because it lives the unspoken universal truth that life is hard and knowing that turns small victories into world-class triumphs—to be followed, of course, by a cosmic horselaugh.

The beauty created by all this madness is odd but authentic. One is particularly thankful for it in a time when the beauty of the city has been so painfully damaged. In late autumn through the winter, as the cold sun is dissolving somewhere in New Jersey, the city lights pop on, and everything feels small and whole and sweet. It is an illusion, but it often lasts the night.

30

WE HAVE AN ENORMOUS INVENTORY OR, WHAT IS THIS THING CALLED LOVE?

In which the author paddles his own canoe down a stream of unconsciousness and discovers the country of his dreams

✶ ✶ ✶

Driving on the highway, I am stuck behind a black delivery truck from East Coast Custom Car. On the back of the truck in bright yellow lettering is a list of things sold at East Coast Custom Car: stereos, alarm systems, bed liners, 4 x 4 accessories, trailer hitches, fog lights, wheels, "and so much more." I make a note to include these items in my accounts, then turn off toward the bay, which, at summer's end, is winter blue already. The powerboats have disappeared. The cormorants swarm in a black mass near the mouth of a creek, their snake heads craning for invisible fish. I watch for a while, slip in a tape of k. d. lang and add these things to my list as well.

Then I drive home, where I make more entries still. In the mail are new pictures of the children. I share a cup of hot chocolate with the dog; the wind kicks up. The fat pine on the front lawn trembles its skirts in the late afternoon; shadows smudge the hedges; day hook-slides into night. I think of high school baseball, then basketball. The orange moon hangs so low it looks as if it is about to fall to earth and bounce.

Here I go again. I am always doing this—taking an inventory of the country, a half-aware accounting that totals up as a feeling of certain, if irrational, affection, a stream of unconsciousness. There's no hard evidence in this list—no passage of a just law, no moment of national courage or generosity, nothing that would stand up in court as a reason for loving the place. Images and memories, mostly. This inventory is getting out of hand. Last week alone I made more than a thousand new entries, and I never erase the old ones. If this keeps up, I will require a dozen ledgers, and even then my accounts will come up short.

Did you know that there is a species of turtle called Kemp's ridley? They are born on a nesting beach in

Mexico (only a few survive) and then swim madly out to sea, where they are carried by the Gulf Stream all the way up to Long Island (it takes three to five years), where they feed for a year on the defenseless spider crab as a training exercise before they take off again and swim down to the Chesapeake Bay area in Maryland, where they eat the much tougher blue claw crab for which the Long Island boot camp has prepared them. Needless to say, they made my inventory.

As did the deer, the full-size antlered stag I saw the other day at dusk, as I was walking down the main street of my Long Island village. Suddenly he stepped out of a driveway, looked ready to panic, saw it was only me, and trotted, head high, down the center of the street.

I put him on the same page as Cole Porter (why not?) who constitutes a huge part of my love of country. Play "In the Still of the Night" and I drop to my knees— the heartache of the internal rhymes of the last lines "Like the moon growing dim, on the rim of a hill, in the chill, still of the night."

As long as I am hearing things, I'll add Ella, always, and Louis, especially when they're singing together, and Joe Cocker and Sarah Vaughan and Frank. I first heard Sinatra on radio. Radio. Fred Allen. Jack Benny. Bob and

Ray. One morning Bob and Ray were creating slogans for license plates and came up with this one: "Kansas— the Gateway to Nebraska." Curled up on the living room rug, I used to listen to *The Shadow*. In one episode, they had to indicate that some time had passed between scenes. "Well, Margot," said Lamont Cranston to his companion, "Here it is, the next day."

I taste A&W root beer. I bite into a double cheeseburger with a holster of fries. (How do I get taste into my inventory?) I'm at my first baseball game. When I was six, the mother of one of the neighborhood kids took a bunch of us to Yankee Stadium. Joe DiMaggio, nearing the end of his career, hit a home run to the opposite field, to the right field stands where we were sitting. "A home run by Joe DiMaggio in your very first game," said my friend's mom. "You'll never forget *that*." At the time of DiMaggio's death, I chatted with Roger Angell, the great baseball writer, and remarked upon that well-known yet unbelievable statistic: 361 lifetime homers, 369 lifetime strikeouts. Angell made the point finer when he noted that in 1941, in 541 at bats, DiMaggio struck out only thirteen times. Then the two of us sighed like kids.

Which takes me to games of catch with my own kids—I have plenty of entries on that. The American game of catch—so un-American, in a way, so calm and uncompetitive. They do not call it a game of throw, though throwing is half the equation. The name of the game puts the burden on the one who receives, but there is really no game to it. Nobody wins or loses. A ball travels between two people, each seeking a moment of understanding from the other, across the yard and the years. To play a game of catch is not like pitching to a batter. You do not throw to trick, confuse, or evade; you want to be understood.

Which brings me to a page on playground basketball in New York, in the summers when I was a teenager. Loping along the white sidewalks that glinted with mica in the sun. The total silence of the early morning, save for the brief musical echo of the ball. Which takes me to a farmhouse we bought in New Hampshire, our first house ($21,000 for sixty acres without water). The local guy with a backhoe leveled a basketball court for me. He asked me if I knew the professor down the road. "He's like you," he said. "Doesn't work."

Which brings me (I never understand these connections) to a hot day in Great Falls, Montana, when I was doing a story on the nuclear missile silos there. A farmer who had leased a corner of his land for one of the silos drove his tractor through a field of malting barley, and I rode with him. He spoke of Vietnam and of Pakistan having the Bomb. He wore a baseball cap to keep off the sun. In the silo, I talked with two young men in the Air Force, both around nineteen. They shared a Diet Pepsi, which rested on the console.

In Los Alamos I met a young woman who made nuclear missiles. In Brooklyn I met a man who made the linings of tunnels. In Norwich, Vermont, I met a calligrapher to whom I gave a beat-up Flexible Flyer and asked him to write ROSENBUD on the top of the sled. He didn't get the bad joke and kept asking me if I was spelling my name right.

Citizen Kane, The Maltese Falcon, Foreign Correspondent. The great last words of *Foreign Correspondent:* "Hello, America. Hang onto your lights. They're the only lights left in the world." *Mr. Smith Goes to Washington. Across the Pacific.* Sylvia Earle, the oceanographer, took me out into the Pacific and showed me humpback whales feeding on krill, and dolphins in motorcycle gang formation. She spoke of larvaceans, and cephalopods like the chambered nautilus, and the *vampyroteuthis infernalis,* the vampire squid from hell, with its salmon-colored body and its sea-blue eyes. "You need to meet fish," she said.

Other great people encountered: the physician and philosopher Lewis Thomas, the poet Sterling Brown, my teacher John Kelleher. Met a prisoner in Attica once. Sy Jackson, African-American, exactly my age then—forty-one. We sat at opposite ends of his cot in his cell, and he told me of a career that started out with a disturbing-the-peace charge when he banged on his girlfriend's door that led to hitting a cop that led to more jail time that led to more fights in prison, and then parole, until he was caught with a gun and sent back to Attica. All those years in prison. On his cell wall he had copied out the poem "Invictus."

The sound of the gate clanking behind me at Attica—must make a note of that. In my Gramercy Park neighborhood of New York, the park has a gate, and only local residents have keys. Beautiful, confining place. Full of eccentrics. Stephen Garmey, minister of the Calvary Church there, told me of a guy who did wood sculptures and took a chunk of a tree home with him from the park that was dying of Dutch elm disease. He called Garmey a few days later and said he felt very sick. He was sure he had Dutch elm disease.

Funny people: Years ago when I was writing a column for the *Washington Post,* Howard Simons, a wonderful, tough, old-school journalist was managing editor. One morning we were in the men's room, standing urinal to urinal, and I asked him, "Howard, why is it that one pronounces the 'n' in the word columnist, but not in the word column? Why isn't it columist?" Howard sighed. "Roger," he said, "I wish I had your problems."

Clever people: One day I heard the columnist Liz Smith report on television: "We have just learned that Claus von Bulow served as the ring bearer in the wedding of Hermann Goering." She paused. "I know it's boring," said Liz. "But we get so few social notes from the Third Reich these days."

Lovely, strong people: Sister Mary Paul of the Center for Family Life in Sunset Park, Brooklyn. She and Sister Geraldine worked a lifetime to serve the needs of the poor neighborhood. She told me, "People call us a charity organization. I don't like the word charity, except in the sense of *caritas*, love. Love is not based on marking people up by their assets and virtues. Love is based on the sense of the mystery of the person. Here we have the privilege of meeting people *in via,* as it is said, on the way. They're on a journey. The gratitude I feel is that I am able to see this particular person at this particular time.

Yet the person remains an unfathomable mystery and is going somewhere I will never know."

Getting late. Gotta stop. How am I going to get this all in? I should hire an accountant. The moon is sky-high now, a small pale eye at the top of the night. A plane blinks by overhead. Fearful thoughts come with planes these days. Still, and always, gratitude to the great, unwieldy country. For the dignity and the struggle. For the strange sweetness, the kindness, the pep, the pluck, the sublime mess. For human courage and turtle courage. For baseball and Satchmo and Groucho and trailer hitches and oceans and alarm systems and dogs and trout and so much more.

ACKNOWLEDGMENTS

⭑ ⭑ ⭑

Not long after September 11, Bob Pattison, my friend and colleague at Southampton College, called and said, "You ought to write a book about why America is worth defending." I asked him why he didn't write it himself, since Pattison would do a beautiful job with this subject. But he is encumbered with modesty. His book would have been better than mine. I am pleased to acknowledge my gratitude to him, as well as my good luck in knowing such a good and thoughtful fellow.

My thanks also and as always to my wife, Ginny, one of the two best editors a writer could have. My reasons for loving her number a lot more than thirty. My other great editor is Jane Isay of Harcourt, who is getting to think more like me than I do. I'm worried about her. That goes for Jane Freeman, too, a remarkable artist who lends me part of her time to put my work into something called a computer.

Amy Cacciola and Danielle Esposito, as part of their charity work, have helped in the research of this book. Soon, these two impressive young women will be famous American novelists. I wonder if they'll miss me.

Gloria Loomis, my agent for twenty-five years, continues to show me irrational patience, for which she, too, has my thanks and affection. My children, by biology and marriage, Carl, Amy, John, Wendy, and Harris, stay out of my way and still say nice, soothing things to me, so I'm grateful to them as well. As for Jessica, our first grandchild, and the one to whom this book is dedicated, I can only tell you that she is shockingly brilliant, stunningly beautiful, astonishingly wise, generous in nature, and exceedingly witty. Did I mention that she can walk?

ROGER ROSENBLATT